Evolution of Cultural Management and Policy in Europe

Since the 1990s, cultural management and policy in Europe have undergone transformative changes. This insightful book offers a comprehensive journey through that evolution, blending historical insights with an analysis of current trends to illuminate the future of the field.

The book also highlights the pivotal role of cultural networks in shaping and advancing culture, creativity, and heritage, bridging academic inquiry with real-world practice. Through a focused case study on the European Network on Cultural Management and Policy, ENCATC, it provides a unique perspective on how networks shape policy and management strategies across Europe.

A must-read for scholars, practitioners, policymakers, and students, this book delivers key insights into the ever-changing landscape of arts and cultural management.

GiannaLia Cogliandro Beyens is Secretary General of ENCATC.

ENCATC Advances in Cultural Management and Policy
Editors: Richard Maloney, *New York University, USA* and
Cristina Ortega Nuere, *3Walks, Spain*

ENCATC has recognized that education in the fields of cultural management and cultural policy cannot and should not be separated from on-the-ground research. Following this stipulation, since its creation, ENCATC has always been very active in pursuing, publishing, presenting, and disseminating research in the fields of cultural management and cultural policy to improve and build upon understanding of cultural management and cultural policy issues. In line with the above-mentioned approach, ENCATC established a series of book publications by research award winners and its members.

The series exists to foster critical debate, publish original cultural management and cultural policy research, and facilitate discussion about cultural management and cultural policy among researchers, educators, scholars, policy makers, and cultural managers. It is also intended to serve as reference material for educators and to support lifelong learning for policymakers and practitioners.

Book Series Publishing Partner
ENCATC European network on cultural management and policy
1, Avenue Maurice
B-1050 Brussels
Belgium
Tel: 0032.2.201.29.12
info@encatc.org; www.encatc.org

European Networks and Cultural Governance
How Culture Makes Policy
Carlotta Scioldo

Evolution of Cultural Management and Policy in Europe
Shaping Culture
Edited by GiannaLia Cogliandro Beyens

For more information about this series, please visit: www.routledge.com/ENCATC-Advances-in-Cultural-Management-and-Policy/book-series/ENCATC

Evolution of Cultural Management and Policy in Europe

Shaping Culture

Edited by
GiannaLia Cogliandro Beyens

Routledge
Taylor & Francis Group
LONDON AND NEW YORK

ENCATC
The European network on cultural management and policy

First published 2025
by Routledge
4 Park Square, Milton Park, Abingdon, Oxon OX14 4RN

and by Routledge
605 Third Avenue, New York, NY 10158

Routledge is an imprint of the Taylor & Francis Group, an informa business

British Library Cataloguing-in-Publication Data
A catalogue record for this book is available from the British Library

ISBN: 978-1-032-97600-6 (hbk)
ISBN: 978-1-032-97601-3 (pbk)
ISBN: 978-1-003-59441-3 (ebk)

DOI: 10.4324/9781003594413

Typeset in Times New Roman
by Apex CoVantage, LLC

Contents

Contributors

Lluís Bonet is a professor of public economy, Director of the Doctoral and the Graduate Programme on Cultural Management at the University of Barcelona, and former president of ENCATC.

GiannaLia Cogliandro Beyens is Secretary General of ENCATC.

Milena Dragićević Šešić is a Prof. Emerita at the University of Arts Belgrade and ENCATC fellowship laureate 2019.

Rod Fisher is an associate lecturer at the Institute for Creative and Cultural Entrepreneurship, Goldsmiths, University of London, and ENCATC fellowship laureate 2021.

Annick Schramme is a full professor at the University of Antwerp (Belgium) and the Antwerp Management School and former president of ENCATC.

Carlotta Scioldo is a lecturer in the Department of Arts and Culture Studies, Erasmus University Rotterdam, and winner of the ENCATC Research Award 2023.

Editorial

GiannaLia Cogliandro Beyens

ENCATC Secretary General

This publication, marking the occasion of ENCATC's 30th anniversary, focuses on two topics that are at the core of ENCATC's mission and vision: firstly, the development of the cultural management and policy discipline to contribute to an inclusive, sustainable, and democratic development of arts and culture for the benefit of society, and, secondly, the promotion of networking in the cultural sector to ensure the evolution of a cultural and creative diverse ecosystem, to contribute to shifts in EU values, frameworks, and institutional governance.

To provide a comprehensive review on these two themes, we have collaborated with esteemed experts in the field, who have shared with us their valuable insights and reflections. As a result, we believe that this publication will certainly contribute to the development of knowledge, to stimulate research, and to provoke debate inside the cultural management and policy community.

First, Annick Schramme, Milena Dragićević-Šešić, and Rod Fisher present reflections on the evolution of cultural management education in Europe and worldwide. Their insights provide a comprehensive overview of this young yet rapidly growing discipline, highlighting its increasing importance over the last decade. They trace its development alongside the professionalisation of cultural organisation management and the rise of cultural policies in the late 20th century. This chapter also explores the recent shift towards entrepreneurial-oriented curricula and the emergence of cultural management as a research-based academic discipline.

Next, Carlotta Scioldo's chapter examines the complex landscape of transnational networks within the cultural and creative sectors. By analysing the evolution of these networks through the lens of public policy, Scioldo reveals the political implications of mainstreaming such practices within the EU context. This approach offers a deeper understanding of the networks' roles and positions them within broader political debates.

Following this, Lluís Bonet discusses the innovative role of cultural management in fostering creativity and innovation in the arts and heritage sectors.

He emphasises the challenges of transforming imaginative ideas into viable projects and highlights the crucial role of cultural managers in promoting and valuing artistic expressions and heritage. This chapter sheds light on the factors that hinder innovation in cultural management, including limited resources, inadequate training, and the fragility of the cultural market.

These contributions perfectly depict the context in which ENCATC has developed and to which it has contributed over the past 30 years. During this time, ENCATC has pursued a visionary mission: to enhance the development of cultural management and policy education and research by promoting networking on a global scale. By embracing innovation and adapting to evolving political, economic, social, and technological landscapes, ENCATC has consistently upheld its foundational values of sustainability, resilience, and inclusivity. The organisation has placed a strong emphasis on fostering collaboration, facilitating knowledge exchange, and supporting professional growth within the cultural sector. Through its diverse initiatives and commitment to engaging with a broad spectrum of institutions and communities, ENCATC has demonstrated its dedication to advancing cultural management and policy in a rapidly changing world.

Since our last anniversary publication five years ago, celebrating ENCATC's 25 years, cultural networks have proven to act as a catalyst for transformative sustainable policy, the creation, development, and sharing of knowledge, and the improvement of innovation in education and practice. As the world faced unprecedented challenges – such as the COVID-19 pandemic or accelerated climate change – cultural networks have provided essential support, facilitating the rapid exchange of information, resources, and innovative solutions. We helped cultural institutions and professionals adapt to new realities, ensuring the continuity of cultural activities and fostering resilience within the sector. The pandemic underscored the importance of cultural networks in maintaining connectivity, collaboration, and community support during times of crisis.

Cultural networks have continuously evolved to face contemporary challenges, and ENCATC has been at the forefront of this evolution. Notably, to name only a few, to endorse and integrate the green transformation and transition in policies and in the day-to-day operations of organisations themselves, as well as to reinforce the capacity of the cultural and creative sectors to meet the objectives of the Green Deal and the 2030 Agenda, ENCATC has designed an annual Academy on sustainable cultural management and policy. Additionally, to bolster research practices and empower researchers, thereby fortifying a competitive European research area, ENCATC has finalised innovative partnerships for the production and open source dissemination of innovative research through scientific publications (such as the present Routledge Book series, or the *European Journal on Cultural Management and Policy*) and has promoted access to data and curated information in the format of quarterly

ENCATC Policy Trackers and through the ENCATC Knowledge Hub. These initiatives exemplify how ENCATC has adapted to meet contemporary challenges and set an example for other networks.

We invite you to join us on this journey, celebrating everyone who has contributed to the development of the cultural management and policy discipline and to the story of cultural networks in Europe and beyond over the past 30 years.

1 Cultural management education and training – historical developments and future perspectives

Honouring 30 years of ENCATC network

Annick Schramme, Milena Dragićević Šešić, and Rod Fisher

1.1 Historical overview

A discussion of the state of cultural management education today should begin with a short history of its development as a field, which is essential to gain an understanding of the challenges and problems faced by cultural managers today. The practice of cultural management is as old as art itself, but the formal academic field devoted to its study and the training of its practitioners is still very young and diversified. Historically, cultural managers (managers of orchestras, theatres, dance companies, museums, etc.) derived their knowledge from on-the-job experience (DiMaggio, 1987). For many, it was their expertise in their particular artistic discipline and their diplomatic skills which made them cultural managers. Others (particularly since the 19th century), such as impresarios, with their endless pursuit of audiences and novelty, drove many arts disciplines to explore new venues, forms, and practices (Kotler & Scheff, 1997; Varela, 2013).

On the other side, throughout the 20th century, socialist movements had strong cultural dimensions, focusing on the fact that the traditional bourgeois cultural institutions were mostly inaccessible for the working class. That is why a new generation of cultural workers (operators, *animateurs socio-culturels*) appeared, mostly in France, Belgium, and Italy, where different movements such as *Travail et Culture* and *Peuple et Culture* were created. Cultural policies of socialist countries needed a large number of cultural professionals for new cultural institutions which were being rapidly established everywhere, even in villages. Also, the post–Second World War period was marked by the countercultural movement that expressed itself mostly through music, arts, and culture. Its new organisations and art collectives searched for new patterns of work (*modus operandi*) which until then did not exist in the

DOI: 10.4324/9781003594413-1

public sector, even less in the private one (squatting abandoned buildings, creating artistic collectives, etc.).

During the Cold War, arts were also used as means for mutual combat, so the profession of cultural operator got its multiple forms, but mostly without a proper academic education. In Eastern Europe, newly created universities of arts and culture were offering both theoretical and practical education, while in the West theoretical education (art history, musicology, aesthetics, etc.) was offered by general universities, and artists were educated at conservatoriums and art schools. Thus, graduated critics, curators, and so on had no opportunity to meet their generation of artists during formal education, and vice versa, and were usually lacking in practical professional knowledge.

In Yugoslavia, which since the 1950s tried to follow its own path of sociopolitical development (not only in politics and economics but in all social spheres), self-governance was applied to culture and education, enabling educational institutions to act independently and create programmes and courses according to their insights about social needs. That is how professors of the Academy for the Theatre, Film, Radio and Television (today the Faculty of Dramatic Arts) in Belgrade had the idea to create a highly original programme: The *Department for Organisers of Cultural Activities*. The Department enrolled its first students in 1961, preparing them to be film and theatre producers, cultural operators, festivals and music managers (the term "manager" was then used only in music, especially folk and popular music), cultural administrators operating at different levels (from ministries to local public cultural institutions), and cultural animators in big companies which offered cultural activities to their workers.[1] Due to the character of Belgrade's art school, the emphasis was on theatre, film, radio, and television production, so students worked in teams with students of other departments (for acting, directing, camera, etc.) on exam projects (theatre plays, films, and radio and TV dramas), which was not possible outside the art school, within university education (i.e. at the Department for Art History of Belgrade University, the students were not able to create/curate exhibitions). This was the first higher education institution in Europe that offered a four-year bachelor diploma in this domain.

The department for the organisation of cultural activities in Belgrade inspired other educational institutions in Yugoslavia and abroad, so the Teachers Training College in Rijeka (now Croatia) opened a similar department, but focused on continuous professional development of cultural animators already employed in companies, while the Faculty of Philosophy in Zadar

1 Not only Yugoslavian companies but all French public companies such as SNCF (national railways) and Renault had offices and programmes for workers' cultural life. In Brazil, SESC cultural centres were financed with 1% from gross salaries in the private sector, so throughout Brazil, SESC cultural centres have taken care of the cultural life and leisure activities of the working class.

(now Croatia) under the same name (OKD – Organisation of cultural activities) offered education mostly for cultural operators in tourism, festivals, and so on. Seeing the success and usefulness of Belgrade's Department, Professor Anatoly Yufit (the Soviet Union) established a similar model in Leningrad in 1967 and after that in seven other theatre schools in the Soviet Union. However, these were not mere copies of the one in Belgrade. Soviet management departments had a different name, and graduates were qualifying with a diploma of a cultural economist. That was, probably, the way to keep this profession as autonomous as possible in a highly ideologised Soviet Union and introduce it easier in the traditional theatre system of dual management, where a director is in fact an artistic director, while a manager is taking care of the economy of an organisation.

In the US, Los Angeles University was the first to introduce theatre production as a study programme at the beginning of the 1950s. The rise of film and theatre industries in post–Second World War California demanded a new type of professional, capable of both managing production and disseminating plays and films all over the world. So, it is not surprising that the 1965 Rockefeller Panel paper was one of the first policy papers to call for a more professional managerial framework for the arts. Their goals for resident professional theatres included making the arts more "business-like" through improvements to administration and fiscal management and selling more tickets through more aggressive and sophisticated marketing (Janetski, 2007). The Rockefeller Panel also acknowledged the need for formal training for arts managers and suggested that higher education institutes should accept this challenge. Thus, the graduate programmes in arts administration emerged in the US with the establishment of Theatre Management programmes at Yale University in 1966 and New York University in 1971 and Arts Administration and Arts Management programmes at the University of Wisconsin–Madison in 1969. The number of programmes grew steadily over the following years, reaching a total of 46 by 2004 in the US alone and doubling to over 80 by 2012. The key word was *administration*, and universities in the US subsequently began offering graduate and postgraduate studies in Arts Administration.

The emergence of these programmes was due to a combination of environmental shifts that had a broad impact on the arts sector (Varela, 2013). Some of these shifts and their consequences include the recession caused by the oil crisis of 1973 followed by a peak in the 1980s; a more significant role for the government in the support of the arts and the obligation to use more formalised grant application procedures; the impact of technological advances (Baumol & Bowen, 1966); and an increasing supply of arts organisations (Kotler & Scheff, 1997). These shifts meant that it was no longer sufficient for arts managers to be merely well versed in their artistic disciplines or have relations with persons in high places. According to Varela (2013), this style of arts management had already become quite obsolete in the 1960s, and by the 1970s, in the US, a new kind of manager was needed. Already in 1987, Paul DiMaggio identified two key areas of expertise required for the emergence of a new generation of arts managers in the US: being versed in seeking and maintaining private support and preserving the public image of the institution to attract audiences and generate revenue. The two principal arenas of activity for arts organisations, management, and artistic discipline came to share equal status. This sea change in priorities led, in turn, to the rise of arts management as a formal academic field (Varela, 2013).

The 1960s were a crossroads for arts organisations throughout the world. Processes of decolonisation and creation of numerous new states brought to the agenda issues of national/local culture and newly created national cultural institutions, from Dakar to Cambodia and Vietnam. On the other side, welfare states of the Global North created ministries for culture in order to make arts and culture more accessible. Cities created and supported numerous festivals, while the countercultural movement, which was at its peak, fought for its own spaces and institutions (from the Woodstock festival and Summer of Love 1967 in San Francisco to numerous squats in Amsterdam, Luxembourg, and Copenhagen). Art administrators and policymakers able to understand different needs of a changing public, commercial, and civil cultural sector were needed everywhere.

In Europe, the situation was even more specific. After recovering from the Second World War, several democratic European countries developed what we now call the "welfare state". This entailed a considerably greater role for government, with arts and culture also seen as part of this social system. Social-democratic governments believed that arts and culture could contribute to the well-being of their citizens. Governmental support for the arts and culture was above all legitimised by its social function.

Another important evolution was the establishment of a separate Ministry for Arts and Culture – distinct from Education – in several European countries. In France, for example, the famous writer André Malraux became Minister for Culture at the end of the 1950s, making arts and culture an autonomous policy domain (Peacock, 1969, pp. 323–235). During the "Golden Sixties", the main goal of the policy was the democratisation of culture through broad dissemination (socially and geographically) and by stimulating participation. However, by the end of that decade, this "top-down" approach was increasingly challenged in some countries as being elitist.

Paradigmatic was the French experience in the 1960s (with André Malraux as the Minister) that focused not only on sociocultural animation but on the creation of the whole network of completely new cultural institutions as well: *maisons de la culture*, *centre d'action culturelle*, *equipements integrees*, and so on. Municipalities and cities, as well as other ministries, accepted and joined these trends, thus networks of Foyer ruraux, Maison des Jeunes et de la Culture, and so on had been created. A new push to the institutionalisation of culture happened with Jack Lang as the Minister in the 1980s, with the creation of *Scenes Nationales* throughout France, *FRAC – Fonds régional d'art contemporain*, and so on. This institutional system demanded more and more highly educated cultural professionals.

Within the wider European context, formal training in cultural management was still not perceived by practitioners as being particularly valuable. Most had been trained and had begun their careers in another era, when the skills required for directors were centred on discipline-specific expertise in the arts (dance, theatre, music, curating, etc.) or in sociology or arts history. It was the government that primarily took care of the financing of the arts, even building many new cultural infrastructures to "bring culture to the people", as part of their democratisation strategy. However, new cultural policies demanded new skills, so the training of cultural operators started to be organised by public authorities. Already in 1959, the Committee for the Cultural Equipment of the Fourth Plan (France) asked for the creation of the Centre for Education of Cultural Animators "to respond to needs after the creation of the first centres for cultural action and houses of culture". The next committee, in 1964, underlined the need for a flexible system of education that could integrate "seminars in cultural centres and houses of culture in full contact with both creators and audiences". The Sixth Plan foresaw the need for the education of 5,000–6,000 cultural animators per year. However, the process was slower than the researchers and professionals in planning committees wanted it to be. The first professional diploma in this area – DECEP (*le Diplome d'Etat de Conseiller d'Education Populaire*) – was issued in 1964 by the State Secretariat for Youth and Sport.[2] In 1975, education for cultural animators was offered already in 18 universities and higher educational institutions whose work was controlled by the Ministry of Education. Five training centres[3] belonged directly to different ministries, 25 were run by non-profit associations, and only 2 were commercial (profit-oriented) (Dragićević-Šešić, 1978). This indicates to what extent cultural professionals in Europe have seen themselves as part of the public sphere or, specifically during the 1960s and 1970s, as part of the cultural counterpublics. Rarely they saw themselves as part of the private sphere.

2 Education was organised by the Ecole Practique de Service Social (est. 1960) and the Training Centre Amities Sociales (1962). A school for free-time animators was opened in 1964, specialising in sociocultural animation in tourism. In 1968, several departments for the two-year education of animators were created in higher education institutions, issuing *Diplome Universitaire de Technologie*. In 1970, a few universities, within their departments for theatre or social studies, opened programmes for cultural animators on all three levels: bachelor, master, and doctoral.

3 Besides the Ministry of Education, which controlled the education of 45% of students, other involved ministries were: Ministry of Culture (0.50%), Ministry of Youth and Sport (23%), Ministry of Public Health (21%), Ministry for Social Affairs (4%), Ministry of Agriculture (3.50%), and Ministry for Tourism (3%). Although it seems odd that the smallest number of students were attending programmes supervised by the Ministry of Culture, practically all animators educated under the Ministry of Education and the Ministry of Youth and Sport were educated for cultural work in a differentiated system of cultural institutions.

Even when they recognised they needed to acquire additional skills, a significant concern for arts and cultural managers was finding sufficient time to take protracted periods away from their organisations to undertake formal training. Short in-service training or modular short courses that provided participants with the opportunity of obtaining credits towards a recognised qualification were seen as options that could respond to the needs of individuals under pressure (Fisher & Mitchell, 1992).

Şuteu (2006) observed that the cultural manager's orientation to society and especially to public cultural policy – and not to the private sector – is typical for the European context. In fact, the common belief during the 1960s was that management and the arts were even incompatible, echoing the ideas of the Frankfurt School thinkers like Horkheimer, Adorno, and Benjamin (Hagoort, 2007). The thought was that the rational mindset of managers would only lead to "massification" and profit-making activities, which stand opposed to artistic integrity, and thus undermine the quality of cultural products (see also Chiapello, 1998). These critical concerns were very strongly felt and are even still present in the minds of many artists and cultural organisations today.

Moreover, during the 1980s, neoliberalist right-wing parties came to power in response to the economic crisis. They wanted to reduce the role of the state, with deregulation, privatisation, competition, return on investment, and sponsorship becoming the key words in the political domain (with Margaret Thatcher the prime minister of the UK and Ronald Reagan the president of the US). In the field of cultural policy, this resulted in a reorientation with respect to the support of arts and culture. Stability may have been a management ideal, but in the arts, it was never easy to predict and control events. However, with the growth in levels of public funding for culture came the demand for greater accountability. Arts administrators and cultural managers in a number of countries were being required to demonstrate to governing authorities that they could manage their budgets effectively in a time of flux (Fisher & Mitchell, 1992). New preconditions were introduced at the micro level, such as budget responsibility, minimum income standards, and the introduction of management skills to deal with this new reality in praxis (Hagoort, 2005). Training was perceived to have a crucial role in helping managers handle change constructively to ensure the health and survival of their organisations in the face of new economic realities (Fisher & Mitchell, 1992). Hence, this need for more management resulted also in the establishment of several training and education programmes in cultural management at different levels in Europe and elsewhere. By the 1990s, arts management in the UK had changed from a profession to an industry, moving from social value to economic value (Watt & Welton, 1990).

In the UK, an early publication, *Arts Administration* (1980), by John Pick, defined the arts administrator as a combination of practical manager, problem-solver, entrepreneur, risk bearer, and idealist. It was Pick who was in charge of the first graduate and postgraduate training in arts administration in the UK. Based at City University, London, it replaced a diploma course that had been initiated at the end of the 1960s in another higher education institution. The Arts Council of Great Britain played an important role in encouraging training in the field and provided financial support for a period. Another early training initiative was launched in 1973 in Vienna by the Institut fur Kulturelles Management at the Hochschule fur Musik und Darstellende Kunst. Elsewhere on the continent, initiatives in France, Germany, Finland, and the Netherlands contributed to this new knowledge and education domain and led to new programmes and training centres. At the end of the 1990s, programmes were also developed in Spain, Italy, Belgium, and some Eastern European countries. Of course, management in and of the arts was not new. What was new was the study of arts management as a discrete subject at an academic level (Hammet, 1989). In the early 1990s, the first handbooks were published in English, which paved the way for the broader participation of arts managers, teachers, and trainers.

The term "Arts Administration" was far less popular in Europe, where new arts and cultural *management* Master's programmes were established only towards the end of the 20th century. Şuteu (2006) noted that the term "management" is more oriented towards strategy and enterprise, and entails a stronger focus on the market as opposed to the hierarchical approach to organisations adopted by arts administration. Moreover, in Europe, the term "cultural management" is much more common than "arts management". Culture not only implies the arts but also heritage, which is a more fundamental element of European culture compared to the US.[4]

In the development of a profession, certain standards have to be fulfilled. The sociology of professions identified several criteria: a large set of skills and competencies; theoretical background and research in an area; existence of a university diploma; professional association (and its relevant activities such as conferences, seminars, and awards); specific professional vocabulary and culture; and the creation of licences and ethical codex. For the arts/cultural manager, most of these criteria have been fulfilled, and the two last ones are still in the process of making. The topic of ethics was introduced during the first conference of the ENCATC network in Warsaw in 1992, but educational programmes, or at least modules, where ethics are elaborated are still rare. Loose associations of researchers in the area started gathering at relevant congresses, notably in 1987 in Hamburg, when Andreas Wiesand and the Zentrum fur Kulturforschung and the CIRCLE network had organised the first international conference on arts management education ("Culture: Administration and Qualification"). It was supported by the Council of Europe,

4 For thoughtful discussions of different aspects of this particular issue, see DeVereaux (2009), Ebewo and Sirayi (2009), Kirchberg and Zembylas (2010), and Kuesters (2010).

European Cultural Foundation, and Federal German Ministry of Culture and attracted researchers and academics from 20 countries, including Australia, Canada, and the USA. It was intended to improve the exchange of information and experiences in training and further education and facilitate greater co-operation and networking between educational institutions and researchers. A survey was initiated for the conference by Wiesand and the ZfK with the intention of ascertaining the extent and nature of arts management and cultural administration training in Europe. Subsequently, however, it became evident that the landscape was changing so rapidly that the survey's findings were being overtaken by events. Consequently, by 1990, the CIRCLE network decided to re-survey all the countries involved, which led to the publication in 1992 of *Professional Managers for the Arts and Culture. Training of Cultural Administrators and Arts Managers in Europe* by Fisher and Mitchell.

Parallel to that, in Yugoslavia, the first conference on arts management and gathering of professors of cultural policy was held in 1988 in Zagreb and Zvečevo (where a Yugoslavian network was created). It brought together academics and alumni from Belgrade (Faculty of Dramatic Arts), Rijeka (Faculty for Industrial Pedagogy), and Zadar (Philosophy Faculty), but also professors of cultural policy from faculties of political sciences in Ljubljana, Zagreb, and Belgrade. One result of the conference was the book largely devoted to the discussion about the profession of cultural organiser: manager, animator, operator, mediator, and worker – as the profession was called (Grbac, 1989).

On an international level, two academics, Yves Evrard from France and François Colbert from Canada, organised the first international conference on arts management as practice (AIMAC) in 1991, while the *International Journal of Arts Management* gave more concrete form to the international educational and research infrastructure. Other international platforms and networks have also appeared, such as the Association of Arts Administration Educators (AAAE) in the US and the European network for cultural administration training centres (ENCATC) in Europe. After the fall of the Berlin Wall in 1989, the Council of Europe, the board of ENCATC, and other relevant European networks (EFAH, CIRCLE, etc.), attempted to support the post-communist cultural sector in Central and Eastern Europe by sharing knowledge and experience, and the European Diploma in Cultural Project Management[5] had an important role in that matter (Deru et al., 2014).

5 As the European Diploma in Cultural Project Management was made for mid-career cultural professionals, it often acted as "training for the trainers" and at least 40 students became academics or trainers in cultural management (from late Snejina Tankovska and Gabriela Tudor, to ENCATC members Margarita Otaegi, Julius Gaidos, Carin Wolf, Ljiljana Simic, Jonathan Woodacre, Violeta Simjanovska, and many more). The Diploma largely contributed to further professionalisation of the sector by initiating the first European network of cultural managers – ORACLE, but also by inspiring students to join other relevant professional networks such as ERICArts, EENC, ECCN, IETM, and Trans Europa Halles.

If we would like to summarise the development of educational programmes for arts/cultural management, at least five periods could be identified:

(1) slow growth (Evrard & Colbert, 2000) from 1961 to 1980 when education was focused on national cultural policy, and skills training that were helping first generations of professional cultural operators to enter public cultural institutions (*maisons de la culture*, arts centres, city theatres and festivals, etc.);
(2) rapid growth phase in-between the 1980s and the 1990s marked with training centres and universities. Education was still focused on national cultural policy, but it started to emphasise marketing and got an international dimension due to the internationalisation of cultural policies (UNESCO conference in Mexico 1982, Council of Europe research endeavours, etc.);
(3) the appearance of networks of educational programmes in the 1990s (AAAE and ENCATC)[6] stimulated internationalisation which was reinforced with political changes (the fall of the Berlin Wall) and the spread of new technologies;[7]
(4) after 2000, stabilisation, consolidation (Varela, 2013), and solidarity strengthened the ENCATC network and its members and partners created numerous joint projects (Policies for Culture and CPEG – Cultural Policy Education Group).[8] The European Cultural Foundation introduced the

6 Despite the fact that members were from different European countries, it was common to learn from and be influenced by the so-called "powerful players" – Anglo-American academic institutions. For Eastern Europeans or Finns, it was common to return after graduation in the UK or the USA and immediately launch similar arts/cultural management programme at home, inviting as guest professors those met abroad (Johansson & Luonila, 2017, pp. 7–8). Columbia College Chicago, Carnegie Mellon University Pittsburgh, Columbia University New York, City University of London, etc. had an important role in these processes. French programmes influenced education only in Romania (ECUMEST) and in Serbia (double-diploma master programme of the University of Arts in Belgrade and the University Lyon II). It was much later that the ENCATC network started to "coproduce" research projects and curricula, involving European peripheries as well (Calliope 1996–98, VANIA 2005–2007), and enabling academics to be more equal in knowledge exchange and contextual, endogenous development of arts/cultural management education.

7 The first ENCATC international project, "Teaching Arts Management in Times of New Technologies", brought together professors and trainers from the University of Lyon, ARSEC (Agence Rhône-Alpes de Services aux Entreprises Culturelles), Sibelius Academy Helsinki, Salzburg International Center for Culture and Management, and the Faculty of Dramatic Arts in Belgrade. The collaboration between University of Lyon II and ARSEC also developed a significant model that showed how arts/cultural management university programmes, long before the Bologna process, have sensed the need to offer training for skills and more practical education which ARSEC was able to provide.

8 These two programmes operated by ECUMEST and the European Cultural Foundation (2000–2006) are paradigmatic for the mutual transfer of knowledge and exchange on solidarity base. The first one engaged educators, practitioners, and policymakers from Balkan countries, while the Cultural Policy Education Group created Baltic–Balkan transversal collaboration (Estonia, Latvia, Lithuania, Poland, Serbia, Romania, and Bulgaria).

Cultural Policy Research Award, now called ENCATC Research Award for recently successfully defended doctoral thesis;

(5) after 2010, academic strengthening resulted in a strong recognition and emphasis on academic research in the area. Numerous research-centred programmes have been created, and already existing programmes introduced doctoral studies, publishing programmes, more research-oriented summer schools,[9] and so on ENCATC enlarged its European scope, created the Journal (2011), took over the Cultural Policy Research Award, established links with academic publishers, and in 2017, on the occasion of 25 years of the network, introduced the ENCATC Fellowship Award (biennial) for a lifetime achievement in arts/cultural management and policy which was for the first time given in 2019.

While programmes were mainly focused on practice in the first several phases, research was becoming more significantly developed in the last phase. This periodisation may be discussed together with changes in cultural policy research and practice. Cultural management teaching was at first dependent on theories coming from cultural studies, cultural policy, and/or cultural development. In the 1960s, cultural development theory and practice needed well-educated professionals, so different training and academic programmes were focused on that (*animation socio-culturelle*, organisation of cultural activities, etc.). Researchers such as Augustin Girard, Bernard Miege, Pierre Gaudibert, and Stevan Majstorovic and policymakers such as Marcel Hicter and Andre Malraux raised interest for the field.

The 1970s marked a huge step from a focus on the democratisation of culture towards a greater awareness of cultural democracy in many countries. In most of the European countries, research centres for cultural development and cultural planning were created and focused on the phenomena of contemporary local and national cultural development (Hermann Glaser, Karla Fohrbeck, Andreas Wiesand,[10] while in the francophone part of Belgium, it was Marcel Hicter, whose heritage is still kept by Association Marcel Hicter for cultural democracy, etc.). Culture was seen as one of the key elements of sociopolitical development that should give voice to every citizen, mostly through associative movements. The Council of Europe, as well as UNESCO, became supporters of reflection and research processes.

9 The research-oriented summer schools in cultural policy and management were developed by Warwick University in 1994, and the next one in 1996, supported by ENCATC, was held simultaneously in three cities: Dresden, Prague, and Wroclaw, with conclusions presented in the border city of Zittau. Unfortunately, this practice was stopped since the leader of the project, Warwick University, left the network to specialise in cultural policy research (not management education and training).

10 The first research project of the Centre for Cultural Research in Köln was about public participation in urban development. The second project already showed interest in the Third World's representation in school textbooks and media.

In the 1980s, the first truly European research projects were realised: "Culture and Working Life: Experiences From Six European Countries" (1980), "Introduction of the Council of Europe Review Programme of National Cultural Policies Starting With France in 1987/88", and "Europe of Regions" (Bassand, 1993, *Culture and Regions of Europe*). First meetings of different organisations led towards the creation of CIRCLE (1980, Strasbourg, and which adopted its name four years later), the European Cultural Forum (1985, Budapest) under the auspices of CCCE (later OSCE), the Eurocircon consortium (1987, Budapest), the Conference of the training centres for arts administration (1987, Hamburg), and the Culturelink Journal (1989, Zagreb). These meetings and numerous related actions paved the way for the creation of strong European and international links in cultural research and art management training (Wiesand, 2002).

In the 1990s, Europe started to celebrate its own unity as the Berlin Wall fell and the Council of Europe took the role of bridging the two divided spheres together. It tried to facilitate transitional processes towards democracy, specifically in the spheres of culture and human rights, especially supporting the creation and activities of different European networks. Indeed, networks became so important, and the Forum of European cultural networks (created in 1988 in Arc-et-Senans) started to have regular meetings in Eastern and Western Europe.[11] Meanwhile, the European Union strengthened its cultural programmes such as the European Cultural Capital programme that, since 1990 in Glasgow, was celebrating not only high culture but the cultures of all cities' communities. In this respect, many sub-disciplines, such as the economy of culture, sociology of culture, and cultural policy, became extremely important in arts/cultural management teaching and research and brought together professors at interdisciplinary conferences (from the international conference on cultural economics in Umea in 1990 to the first ICCPR conference in Bergen in 1999).

Following the end of a bipolar world with the collapse of communism in Eastern and Central Europe, UNESCO, in conjunction with the United Nations, saw an opportunity to explore the significance of culture in the context of development and globalisation. It established a World Commission on Culture and Development to consider how policy for culture (defined broadly as "ways of living together") could be rethought. The Commission commenced its work in 1993 when value systems appeared to be breaking down and the notion of progress without limits had become an illusion as the gulf between the "haves" and "have-nots" was seen to be widening. The Commission sought evidence globally, and, encouraged by the Swedish Government in particular, the Council of Europe set up a European Task Force on Culture and Development as a contribution to the Commission's work. In common with the World Commission, the European Task Force sought to explore ways that

11 Meetings were held in Peles in 1993, in Krakow in 1996, in Brussels in 1997, etc.

culture could be moved to centre stage. However, unlike the Commission, the members of the Task Force were all involved in the arts and culture, whether as researchers, arts council staff, policy advisers, managing festivals, and so on, and most also lectured on arts and/or cultural policy in academia. The Commission's report, *Our Creative Diversity* (World Commission on Culture and Development, 1995), published in late 1995, describes a number of challenges that require a fundamental review of cultural policies and sets out an international agenda for action. The central themes of *In from the Margins*, the report of the European Task Force on Culture and Development (1997), were two interlocking priorities: to bring dispossessed and disadvantaged Europeans in from the margins of society and cultural policy in from the margins of government. A key contention of *In from the Margins* was that ministries with cultural portfolios in many countries will remain impotent in the face of macro developments unless their relative isolation is ended and formal interdepartmental mechanisms are established to make the most of the multiple interactions between culture and social and economic development (i.e. joined-up government). While the European report complemented the World Commission's report, it also existed as a stand-alone document as it was able to be more specific in its more than 70 recommendations. It provides a rich assessment of the cultural environment and analysis of trends and cultural policies in Europe, as well as identifying areas that need to be redirected. Both reports were discussed at UNESCO's Intergovernmental Conference on Culture and Media Policies held in Stockholm in 1998. The two reports provide (and some would argue continue to provide) an abundant source of material for discussion in academia, not least in encouraging consideration of culture in a broader sense.

From 2000 onwards, the ENCATC network had more and more research activities, and its annual meeting turned into the research conference (2001, St. Petersburg), which every year posed a specific topic and asked academics for their research contributions. Together with AIMAC biennial conferences (since 1991), it became the major conference devoted not only to arts/cultural management as such but also to education and training for it.[12] ENCATC also regularly organised students' conferences (2004–2009) and, since 2008, the Young Researchers' Forum on Cultural Policy (today known as the Young and Emerging Researchers' Forum on Cultural Management and Policy). In this decade, the interests of the network became diversified towards leadership, intercultural dialogue, creative industries, the economy of culture, entrepreneurship, cultural diplomacy, and so on.

12 Some of the ENCATC conference topics were *From Rulebooks to Kite Flying* (Dartington, 2002), *Competence in Diversity – Diversity in Competence* (Bratislava, 2006), *Intercultural Dialogue and Project Management: New Training Programmes in a Context of Major Challenges* (Lyon, 2008), *Rethinking Education on Arts and Cultural Management* (Antwerp, 2013), *Cultural Management Education in Risk Societies – Towards a Paradigm and Policy Shift* (Valencia, 2016), etc.

In the next decade (2010–2022), these research activities were complemented with annual research sessions held within the ENCATC Congress and Annual Policy Debates held every year in Brussels or Antwerp since 2011. Very important were academies on culture in external relations (since 2012) and international study tours that took academics far beyond Europe (New York 2013; Shanghai 2014; Boston 2016; Abu Dhabi, Sharjah, and Dubai 2017). To what extent ENCATC had intensified its activities is seen by numerous workshops, seminars, debates, and conferences, complemented with annual master classes in festivals and events management, creative luxury industries, leadership, and digital tools for managers. In addition to those events, numerous Breakfast Training sessions (more than 20 held in Brussels) and Cultural Happy Hours (around 40 held in Brussels, Paris, Venice, and Spain) have also been organised. The increased academic importance of ENCATC as a network can be seen in a number of ENCATC-labelled events, a practice that started in 2016 and supported 51 member organisations until today.

After these intensive two decades in the new millennium, one could say that the field of Arts/Cultural Management in Europe and Arts Administration in the US (as well as in Australia and throughout the world) started to be considered as a new discipline, with its own body of knowledge to be studied and taught, conferences, seminars, workshops, publishing programmes, labels, and awards.

1.2 The specificities of arts/cultural management

Within the knowledge domain of management, we can distinguish a number of very different theories and models specific to cultural management. Taken as a whole, the scientific knowledge base that is specific to cultural management is rather limited compared to that of general management.[13] Many authors who advocate a clear distinction between general management and cultural management do so on the basis of a distinctive or "deviant" application of management models and theories (Verbergt & De Bruyne, 2015). However, Evrard and Colbert (2000) argued that the differences between management in general and arts management in particular may in many ways not be that great and that just as neurology and cardiology are sub-disciplines of medicine, cultural management should be considered a sub-discipline of management.

13 The first group of these concerns the value of culture, which is variously seen as different from, broader than, or even reducible to economic value equations (see e.g. Klamer, 1996, Hutter & Throsby, 2008, Snowball, 2008). Gielen et al. (2014) give an overview of all empirical evidence of the value of culture. Evrard and Colbert (2000) and Noordman (2010) stress that value in arts and culture is experiential, thus immaterial and specific in the sense that it does not diminish after use. The second theory of note is Baumol and Bowen's law on cost disease, the productivity lag that is inherent to the live performing arts. A third group consists of leadership theories that are specific to artistic leadership (Hagoort, 2005).

Nevertheless, we need to be aware that there were no theoretical reasons for starting new cultural management education programmes in Europe. It was a number of rather practical concerns that drove universities to create cultural management programmes, such as the growth and professionalisation of cultural organisations and the increasing complexity of their environment (Noordman, 1993). To this, we could also add numerous cultural policy demands on both national and international levels for better implementation of cultural policies by highly educated professionals. Contrary to business management, arts/cultural management relies, both in theory and in teaching, on cultural policy, even when, sometimes, it is implicit. It is not strange that cultural management teaching started in Europe in the 1960s in the countries with important public cultural policy, whether governmentally led or arm's length (Yugoslavia, France, and the UK).

Kuesters (2010) proposes the use of theoretical frameworks that see arts managers as liaising between the worlds of finance and the arts. Brkić (2009) relied on the metaphor of the Janus head, arguing that cultural management education should include both artistic or cultural education *and* managerial education, with its basis remaining cultural. An ability to shift between the two logics, the artistic-cultural and the entrepreneurial (market-oriented and/or institutional/policy-oriented) is a skill that cultural managers must master if they are to fulfil their role as both a "mediator" and a "companion" (Bendixen, 2000). The companion role is comparable to that of a pianist accompanying a singer. It is a subtle game of leading and following, and vice versa, with trust between the parties also very important. In the end, however, everyone is aware that it is the singer who is the star (Verbergt, 2015).

On the basis of this Janus syndrome perspective, Brkić (2009) concludes that a simultaneous look at general management and the arts is essential to the success of an arts management education programme. Arts managers need to be acquainted with both banks of the river, as well as with the techniques needed to build solid, beautiful, and "challenging" bridges. Besides these two aspects, the ENCATC Summer School in 1996 identified one more important role of a manager – that of a mediator between arts and community. "That is not merely between the artist and the audience, but also between artist and non-audience" (Wesner & Palka, 1997, p. 76). That indicates major differences between the *logics of business management and cultural management.* It can be said that arts/cultural management is a passion-driven sector in the money-driven world (Deru et al., 2014). The logic of business management is different from the logic of cultural management, unless we discuss creative industries in countries whose market enables their strong profitability. The major difference concerns the fact that business management is profit-based, while arts/cultural management is value-based (arguably most of cultural entrepreneurship aims towards new value and art creation that does not necessarily have to be profitable). Business management creates products for the market, while cultural management creates art works or cultural projects for the community. The success of the first is measured with quantitative data, efficiency, productivity, and rentability, while the success of the second is measured by qualitative analysis of experience, effectiveness, influence, and impact. To do that, a business manager is trying to "kill" its competition, while a cultural manager is trying to partner with or even support its "competition". There are numerous other differences that were identified in the business behaviour of the two: in most of the cases, business management is place non-specific (factories can be anywhere in the world), while success is guaranteed mostly by the newest technologies. On the other hand, cultural management often is *genius loci* specific, and success mostly depends on people, not on technology. Entrepreneurship in the first case is market-driven, based on feasibility studies and risk assessment, while arts/cultural entrepreneurship is producer/curator/artist-driven, based on an idea and ambition to contribute to the art scene or in a community. It can be obvious from the start that this entrepreneurial idea might not be market successful but can contribute towards the well-being of people, or, even more often, just to enable the artist or artists collective to express themselves. It shows that cultural management is thinking beyond market and market-related income and that the logic of arts/cultural marketing is more the logic of audience development than of market development.

Aware of that, many departments for arts/cultural management have used several multifunctional strategies: internationalisation (networking), community involvement, lobbying and advocacy for better cultural policies, transforming themselves from institutional to project logic, introducing research, experiments, and innovation, examining interdependence of openness and intersectoral crossings with the development of new ethics of responsibility of contemporary cultural institutions (gender equity, openness to marginal social groups, involvement in decolonising and reconciliation processes, and advocating for human rights and freedoms of artistic expression). Thus, ethics of solidarity, care, and empathy, considered in a larger social context, have started to replace the narrow-conceptualised ethics of cultural management focused only on responsibility towards artists and audiences.

1.3 Education in cultural management

It is only recently that the literature has investigated the nature and logic of cultural management curricula and programme structure. Educational science defines four types of competences: knowledge, skills, insight, and attitudes (Bloom, 1956; De Block & Saveyn, 1985; De Block & Heene, 1992; Hauenstein, 1998; Whitley, 1989, 1995). From this perspective, Mintzberg's definition of management as a practice that combines knowledge, craft, and insight to understand the differences between general management and cultural management is very relevant.

Firstly, although the scientific knowledge of management is clearly one of the foundations of the practice of cultural management, an overly narrow scholarly focus on the scientific aspect and on scientific research in graduate programmes will not contribute to preparing graduate students for a career as a cultural manager. Secondly, management as a practice is also a craft, for which the main learning mode is experience. Graduate study programmes in cultural management that focus on experience, for example, through internships or project-based learning, produce students that are better prepared for the labour market. Thirdly, almost all of the qualities that distinguish arts and cultural management from general management are related to the "vision" or "insight" that managers deploy in their specific work environment, and that is a far broader domain than the scientific base of general management. A more intense field-specific but also interdisciplinary type of education is required to prepare managers to cope with the huge number of challenges in the cultural and creative sectors (Verbergt & De Bruyne, 2015; Lampel et al., 2000).

A survey carried out in 2014 at the University of Antwerp (Belgium) among cultural management graduates over 14 academic years supports the view that cultural management education needs to foster the acquisition of experience and insight into the "bridging" relationship between management and arts and cultural practices (Verbergt & De Bruyne, 2015). The qualitative data from the 2014 survey on the curriculum elements that were perceived as important for employment support the principle of including practical experience in education. The practical internship – which is combined with research for a Master's thesis – was found to be the second most important element after the practice-based course "Cultural Management Forum" (in which managers are invited as guest speakers).

Both in the domains of arts administration and arts management education (so, for policymakers, regional and city cultural officers, researchers in the domain, as well as for future arts/cultural managers, practitioners, and operators), the practical dimension is of extreme importance. Both have to be prepared to act as cultural analysts, policymakers, evaluators, lobbyists, and advocates for programmes and policies that will endorse the arts and cultural sector. Therefore, in all types of schools and universities for administrators and managers – art, media, and design schools; business schools; teacher training colleges; schools for social sciences; or schools for political sciences and communication – the vocational dimension of education is being underlined.

Art and design schools always had practical, vocational education, and their advantage is that students of arts/cultural management can immediately foresee, conceptualise, and have joint projects with artists. Very often, international students' art festivals are created (Brno, Bratislava, Belgrade, Casablanca, etc.). As most of these schools are members not only of ENCATC but of the ELIA (European League of Institutes of the Arts) network as well, they were launching practice-based PhDs and opening possibilities for master and doctoral students of arts/cultural management to opt in-between practice-based and research-based thesis (including curation). If arts/cultural management training was developed within a business school, such as in Burgundy School of Business (Dijon) or HEC Paris, it is habitual to have all types of practices, but implemented within the cultural sector. The third type of schools, teacher training colleges, that host cultural management programmes were always using practice-based education, including arts practices such as theatre in education or drama in education, and sending students on internships. As previously mentioned, at the Teachers Training College in Rijeka (Croatia), a very special vocational programme that had been established in the 1970s for cultural animators in (self-governed) companies was closed in the beginning of the 1990s because it was "accused" for ideologically belonging to communism (see section "Regional Differences in Arts/Cultural Management Education Development"). Programmes and methods for arts/cultural management developed in schools for social sciences depend on the type of a school's department that offers such education. Departments for history of arts, anthropology, or archaeology developed masters in heritage management (tangible and intangible), while departments for sociology and social work tend to have programmes related to developmental studies of local, community development, or international developmental policies. The first one might be more practice-oriented, mostly linking students to heritage institutions and sites, while the second ones sporadically have opportunities to organise study tours and research projects. Cultural management programmes within these departments are more academically oriented, stimulating students to do research-based masters and continue their academic education. Finally, in the fifth group of schools – for political sciences and communication – cultural management programmes might be extremely diverse – from those oriented towards cultural policymaking on different levels to those related to cultural diplomacy and international cultural affairs.

Arts/cultural management programmes are collaborating not only within the same group of schools but are open for sharing their know-how in joint projects with different types of agents. Specific knowledge of making policy recommendations enables these departments to be partners in research that relates to heritage, tourism, political science, communication, and even neuroscience.[14]

1.3.1 Regional differences in arts/cultural management education development

Arts/cultural management education and training programmes are as diverse as jurisdictions across Europe and the world and are heavily influenced by the status of the arts and cultural sector in a society and the legal status of a university (complete autonomy in delivering degrees, or state-centralised

14 Horizon project ARTIS 2020–2025 (Art and Research on Transformations of Individuals and Societies, ID: 870827) joins empirical approaches from psychology, neuroscience, and phenomenology with the intent of conducting a series of investigations that identify specific types of experiences with art, and to result in policy recommendations to EU and national cultural policymakers, as well as to galleries and museums. Different university departments, from neuroscience to cultural management and policy, are partners in this project.

system). In the Anglo-American world, culture is often seen as independent, part of the private sector, depending on entrepreneurialism and philanthropy, while policies are just a corrective to the injustices of the art(s) market. At the same time, universities and, since 1992, polytechnics can award their degrees autonomously (Şuteu, 2006, p. 103). Although in the United Kingdom the role of arts councils might be crucial for arts production and development, all arts institutions are pushed to justify as much as possible their existence in the market. Thus, the meaning of creative industries incorporated all arts, from those that were traditional parts of cultural and creative industries (film, music, publishing, etc.) to those that in most environments can survive only with public subsidies (theatres, contemporary dance, visual arts, etc.).

As Suteu remarks, "when compared to the British model, the French system is one of centralised decision making in terms of awarding degrees . . . while, in terms of content, France is very much addicted to the notion of learning as a value in itself, compared to the pragmatic and accountability oriented Anglo-Saxon approach" (Şuteu, 2006, p. 105). As she further claims, management skills are not important as much as social cohesion, human rights, and development, and among skills most valued are analytical thinking and critical reflection. All that has deeply influenced the diversity of arts/cultural management and administration educational programmes. Consequently, the majority of students who apply for these programmes come from upper middle-class backgrounds and have varied social and educational trajectories, with diversified strategies and expectation of a future job, "dreaming" of the multiple forms of gratification that jobs in the cultural sector will allow. Mostly students quote social prestige conferred by the cultural world, the dynamic and varied activities whose results are easily seen and publicly enjoyed, an opportunity to leave a legacy in society, freedom in a workplace, and work for a common good that brings moral satisfaction of helping out both artists and society (Dubois, 2013, p. 119).

In Spain, Portugal, and Italy, cultural management education took diverse forms: from training institutions to universities with programmes focused on diverse needs of society. The best examples might be found in Spain, where the University of Barcelona has developed master programmes which also attracted numerous students from Latin America, the University Deusto Bilbao focused on cultural tourism, while the University of Valencia put emphasis on the cultural economy.

In Northern Europe, culture was always seen as an important space of safeguarding national language and identity, but in the context of welfare state cultural policies have been developed to adequately address the whole territory of the country. Thus, regional cultural operators and regional arts councils have played an important role in ensuring the possibility for every citizen to participate in cultural life. Strong cultural infrastructures were created, and the fact that culture is part of public interest and public value was never questioned. However, Nordic countries were among the last ones to create educational programmes for cultural managers. Each country usually has only few such programmes which originated from continuous professional development courses (e.g. *Nätverkstan* Goteborg and Sibelius Academy Helsinki).

In Central and Eastern Europe, administration and management programmes were linked to art schools (drama and film), as was the case in Yugoslavia and the Soviet Union. Since the 1990s, university systems have been facing important new challenges because the transition processes have not yet been accomplished (neither for the countries nor for their educational systems), but the new demands were already at stake – the Bologna convention and Lisbon convention were demanding harmonisation of all European national higher education structures (introducing ECTS, mobility of students and educators, three-cycle system, interdisciplinarity, employability, quality assurance, etc.). Moreover, that was a difficult switch from a completely state-supported framework to the mixed system of financing, where a small but crucial part of the funding, which guarantees development and quality of university teaching, had to come from students themselves. De-etatisation of public educational services is questionable in countries whose economies had not yet mounted the transition and lack a minimum degree of sustainability and where the majority of the population is near the poverty line. During the 1990s, three periods can be identified reflecting those changes: (1) a return to "national" cultural values (identity questioning) and rejection of the communist tradition (even rejection of the institutions and curricula created during the period of communism, regardless of their real meaning and impact) (Varela, 2013); (2) the will to pursue European trends and strive for modernisation – a period of acceptance of proposed models (Council of Europe – Mosaic, PHARE trainings, NGO training development, etc.); (3) the revitalisation and reform of curricula – a period of creation of "joint ventures" in education – introduction of the ECTS system, exchange, and so on. Of course, these changes were differently implemented and with a different speed in five regions: Baltic, Central Europe, Southeast Europe (Balkans), Eastern Europe, and Caucasus. The efforts of the Council of Europe (grants for the European Diploma in Cultural Project Management organised by Marcel Hicter Brussels, grants to Central and Eastern European academics to attend ENCATC conferences, mobility grants for cultural managers 1990–2001, and MOSAIC programme training for continuous professional development of cultural administration 1996–2003) that were mostly linked to cultural policy, management, and cultural administration field contributed to the relatively quick development of arts/cultural management education. The foreign cultural institutes and numerous cultural diplomacy programmes helped those processes by giving grants to study arts management in their countries, or organising seminars and summer schools such as the Amsterdam Summer University programme for cultural management and the summer school of Salzburg International Center for Culture and Management. The Soros Foundation was also instrumental in stimulating cultural entrepreneurship and management. The first course in cultural management was organised in Belgrade in 1996 for cultural officers and staff of the Soros Centers for Contemporary Arts and arts and culture coordinators from the whole region (from Baltics to Central Asia), and later numerous programmes for performing arts managers and festival managers that have been held in Budapest and throughout the region. The Central European University in Budapest organised its first summer schools for innovative cultural policy and management in 1999 and 2000, gathering regional academics from Zagreb, Belgrade, Sofia, Moscow, Bucharest, and so on and training cultural operators from the Baltic countries to the Caucasus. This later resulted in the CEU cultural policy education programme ("policy stream"), specifically designed for students from Central and Eastern Europe (course director Dragan Klaic). However, in each of the regions, the trajectory to develop those programmes was different. While in some countries of Central Europe, as well as in countries of the former Yugoslavia, this education was contextualised and based on research, in many other countries of the region, curricula were "universal", and their implementation still heavily depends on foreign guest lecturers who are rarely aware of the cultural context and political and legal system in which a cultural manager has to operate.

Unfortunately, Eastern European colleagues that have been extremely active in ENCATC, ELIA, and other cultural networks of Europe have slowly withdrawn due to non-favourable policies towards Europeanisation processes in their countries (Russia and Belarus), or due to the lack of funding for such mobility (Caucasus countries, Mongolia, etc.).

It seems that the ENCATC network is aware not only of those issues (rethinking to launch again the Tomasen Fund for mobility of Eastern European academics) but also of the need and necessity to reinforce a European knowledge base for cultural management, offering the possibility for publishing in its cultural journal and book series, giving awards for best projects, and so on. Numerous members of ENCATC are supported to present their projects to European programmes (Horizon 2020, Erasmus+, Creative Europe, COST, Marie Sklodowska Curie postdoctoral fellowship, etc.), collaborating mutually and with other academic and civil society partners.

1.4 Curricular structure of cultural management programmes

We will now look into the curricular structure of some other cultural management programmes. Brkić (2009) distinguishes four types of curricula: those that copy directly from business management; those that focus on the technological process of producing artwork; those that link cultural management and cultural policy; and those that take an entrepreneurial approach to arts management, connecting it to issues of creativity and innovation. Concerning the number of programmes, we can rely on the figures from ENCATC. The network has about 130 members from 41 countries (87% from Europe, 6% from the US, 3% from Latin America, 3% from Asia, and 1% from Africa). Higher education institutions account for 64% of the members, and training centres 20%, the remainder coming from arts organisations, public authorities, and artists. The German website www.artsmanagementnetwork.net has listed 152 graduate and postgraduate study programmes, with 96 (63%) containing the word "management" in their title and 27 (18%) the word "administration". Of this latter group, 17 are taught in the US. Two educational institutions offer a degree in "arts administration and management".[15] In the US in 2004, 40 of 46 existing graduate arts management programmes were members of the AAAE, the prime association for arts administration education. By 2012, the number of graduate programmes had risen to 82, of which 56 were full members of AAAE. To qualify for full membership, programmes must "have a designated director, confer a graduate or undergraduate degree in arts administration, have an identifiable and published arts administration curriculum, and have a record of conferred degrees over at least a three-year period" (AAAE, cited in Varela, 2013).

The top four elements resulting from the research of Virela required by at least two-thirds of the programmes were marketing (88.6%); experiential learning, including internships and production labs (86.4%); overview of arts management programmes (79.5%); and policy, including advocacy (79.5%). Following these, fund development, accounting, financial management, law, strategic planning, research, and art courses were also identified as core subjects in the field.

Comparing the descriptions given by respondents based on the survey at the University of Antwerp about the usefulness of management education in their current job, three main topics stand out: that teamwork is necessary in order to finish tasks (as in professional life); the provision of an overview of different management processes and management domains; and the deep insight offered into the specific structure of the sector (policy, legislation, and subsidies). The top seven (of 11) competences evaluated positively by the alumni of the University of Antwerp were: learning to work effectively in a team; being able to work in an entrepreneurial manner; using skills within a network; reflecting more readily on your work and on oneself; translating reflections into constructive activities; having insight into understanding/implementing scientific knowledge in cultural management and undertaking

15 The website lists three institutions that offer master programmes in arts entrepreneurship, all based in the U.K. or the Netherlands.

critical reflection; and processing and synthesising scientific management literature (Verbergt & De Bruyne, 2015).

These findings suggest that there is a clear understanding in the field of the importance of instructing students in applied management theory. In key areas such as marketing, law, and financial management, more programmes are pursuing an arts-specific approach rather than applying straightforward business theory. There are only a few programmes in the US that are heavily business-oriented or require a very strong artistic core discipline. Thus, an extended focus on arts/cultural management programmes seems to be developing.[16]

Unfortunately, no overall empirical qualitative analysis of cultural management programmes in Europe has yet been undertaken. However, UNESCO and ENCATC in 2003 had made the book as inventory, but also there were some efforts of analysing European arts management programmes in their international dimension (Fisher & Karpodini-Dimitriadi, 2007). In the late 1990s and in the early new Millennium, there was a marked increase in cross-border engagement in Europe as arts and cultural organisations sought to achieve economies of scale through co-productions, jointly curated work, or exploratory projects. Although higher education programmes in arts and cultural education may have taught project management, there was increasing concern that too few related these to the additional complexities of running transnational cultural co-operation initiatives. With some financial assistance from the European Commission's Leonardo da Vinci programme, four organisations (Foundation Marcel Hicter, Cupore, International Intelligence on Culture and Evremathia, together with information and data gathered from ENCATC) collaborated in a two-year initiative (VANIA) to examine if and how validation and certification standards could be established for training in transnational cultural co-operation projects. Arguably the report, *Training in Transnational Cultural Co-operation Projects; Reflections and Challenges on Validation and Certification* (Fisher & Karpodini-Dimitriadi, 2007), deserves to be better known.

Even in the US, it was only in 2013 that an analysis took place. One of the reasons for this could be that the programmes are perceived to be too diverse to be investigated and classified. Nevertheless, Varela (2013) found that the field was not as diverse as it was perceived to be by directors and practitioners. Moreover, she concluded that there is a common understanding among the academic programmes in the US of what critical skills are needed in the field of arts management.[17]

16 DiMaggio's (1987) key areas of expertise in arts management – seeking and maintaining private support and preserving the public image of the institution to attract audiences and generate revenue – seem to be reflected in the majority of programme offerings.

17 Most of the arts management programmes in the US are housed in schools of art, but most combine course requirements from a variety of colleges and schools. Only 26% are a full programme at master's level.

Although European arts management development has been discussed at conferences from a comparative perspective (Debrecen 1995; 1999, Belgrade 1997, as well on numerous ENCATC General Assemblies like those in Torino 1996, Bilbao 1997, and Paris 1999), sometimes devoted specifically to developments in CEE including Russia (Dragićević Šešić 1997; Wesner & Palka, Eds 1997; Dragićević Šešić 2003; Dragićević-Šešić, 2009; Dietachmair & Ilić. Eds. 2015), most articles and books covered developments in the West European cultural realm, with interesting articles on particular programs at European universities (Kuhle et al., 2015). In what follows, we outline a selection of relevant discussion points and challenges for cultural management programmes in the future, derived from the literature and evolutions in the field:

> *Today, cultural managers must work in very dynamic, uncertain, and rapidly changing environments. Some of the important shifts they are confronting include a financial crisis and a decrease in funding, an extremely diverse society, and the increasing impact of digitisation and globalisation. Cultural management programmes should take into account these new evolutions to better prepare students for the labour market:*
>
> - Strategic Marketing: *in Europe, as in the US, strategic marketing remains one of the main topics of cultural management programmes. Arts organisations require a supply-side marketing approach (Evrard & Colbert, 2000; Bendixen, 2000). Fillis (2006) describes how the arts demonstrate the implications of ignoring market demand and customer wishes. The arts and the cultural sector must realise that the most fundamental relationship is that with the public. Cultural institutions must be places where intercultural and interdisciplinary cultural dialogue takes place. In order to make the right strategic decisions, it is very important to find and know* "your audience". *Knowing how to use social media or finding other innovative ways of involving the public is also a real challenge for cultural managers today. Strategic cultural management was spread first in Eastern Europe,*[18] *and then throughout the world due to efforts of foreign institutes such as the British Council and Goethe Institute, but also HIVOS and other organisations that are focusing on social development. Thus, the first training for the trainers in arts/theatre management was held in India in 2010, while ECF, together with Al Mawred Al Thaqafi, began to educate trainers*

18 To enumerate just a few that were specifically targeted CEE cultural operators: Cultural Managers from Central and Eastern Europe. International Cultural Management Course, 2011/2012, Germany; European Diploma in Cultural Project Management 2010/11; Gulliver Connect 2009; European Atelier for Young Festival Managers 2009, 26 April–3 May 2009, Varna, Bulgaria; International Summer University for Arts Management, 21 July–9 August 2008, Salzburg, Austria; The Kennedy Center Fellowship Program for Arts Managers, May–September 2008/2009, Washington, DC, USA.

for Arab countries since 2005, while foreign institutes are still focusing only on cultural professionals (Dragićević-Šešić & Mihaljinac, 2020).

- Leadership *is also receiving increasing attention in the context of arts and cultural management programmes. Leaders in arts and culture face specific challenges: managing and leading creative personnel and processes (DeFillippi et al., 2007) means dealing with leadership paradoxes, such as finding a balance between artistic and management goals and between stimulating collaborators' autonomy and setting up functional teams (Andriopoulos, 2003; Kolsteeg, 2014). Hagoort (2005) and Şuteu (2006) list an entire set of specific values of relevance to cultural leaders, including human rights-related, ethical, social, democratic, and idiosyncratic artistic values. Such leaders must be able to understand and critically respond to an unpredictable and rapidly changing environment.*
- Internationalisation: *the context in which cultural managers work is definitely international/global. Gaining intercultural competences should be an integral part of an actual cultural management programme (Mandel, 2015). In January 2015, the German Association of Cultural Management organised its yearly conference on this topic and the Arts Management Newsletter devoted an issue to this (N°122). With regard to globalisation and the differentiation of the cultural sector, the important skills nowadays are how to manage different kinds of projects and to create a career out of short-term employments. This includes aspects like intercultural communication and – since glocalisation is coming along with globalisation – insights into international cultural infrastructures, and social and political circumstances. However, dealing with cultural diversity within the local context is also a real challenge. Cultural policy is becoming increasingly decentralised and the urban environment is the ecosystem where cultural actors engage with each other.*
- Entrepreneurship: *finally, the rise of cultural entrepreneurship as an education and research domain that is closely linked with and interrelated to cultural management education. Although Busenitz et al. (2011) found that entrepreneurship research has gained greater legitimacy and its rightful place within major management journals over the past two decades, a generally accepted definition of entrepreneurship in the research community is still lacking (Brixy et al., 2008; Parker, 2009). This is even more true for the field of entrepreneurship within the cultural and creative sectors. However, one can distinguish at least two important definitions. Firstly, entrepreneurship can refer to owning and managing a business on one's own account and at one's own risk (the occupational notion of entrepreneurship). Secondly, entrepreneurship can refer to* "entrepreneurial behaviour", *in the sense of incorporating economic opportunities (the behavioural notion of entrepreneurship) (Brixy et al., 2012). From our perspective, the latter is the most interesting to investigate. But, seeing entrepreneurship as the panacea only for economic health of cultural organisations is also limited.*

> *Entrepreneurship, seen more broadly as an engine of development, as a flywheel for innovation in the cultural field has created both profit and non-profit endeavours that are important for the creative sector ecosystem (Dragićević-Šešić, 2020).*

One of the main reasons for the rise of the concept of "cultural entrepreneurship" is the changing political, social, and economic environment since the end of the 1990s, which will be elaborated below.

1.5 Creative industries on the political agenda

The first shift took place in the UK at the end of the 1990s,[19] with the creative industries coming onto the political agenda. The catalyst was a statement by the Labour government, which was looking to identify new sectors that could fuel economic prosperity as an alternative to the old industrial job engines of steel and finance. They observed that creative activities such as architecture, design, fashion, and some art productions were creating new industrial-scale movements. These industries contributed almost 8% of the UK's GDP and employed more than 2 million people. What was even more important was that the figures showed an increasing trend (DCMS Report, 1998), in contrast to the old industry sectors. It was clear that these industries were based on the individual quality of (artistic) creativity and that there was huge potential. The publication of Richard Florida's *Creative City* in 2002 also had a huge impact on city governments. According to Florida, the creative class would foster the local economy and increase the attraction of the city. National and local governments became aware of the potential richness of the creative industries and started to develop their own strategies (Hagoort, 2010; Pratt, 2013).

On a global level, two studies went on to illustrate the global impact of the creative industries: the European Commission Green Paper on the creative industries (2009) and the UN Creative Economy Report 2008, which described the creative economy as one which is led by the potential for creativity and innovation to promote social prosperity worldwide.

Almost every European country has developed its own definition of the creative industries over the last ten years and has undertaken its own economic impact analysis (almost 3% of GDP in Europe). At all political levels, governments actually believe that the cultural and creative industries are fundamental to advancing prosperity, inclusiveness, and sustainability. Most of the definitions also include the traditionally subsidised sectors of arts and heritage (Throsby, 2010). For this reason, the European Commission no longer uses the term "creative industries" but speaks of the cultural and creative "sectors", making this inclusive approach explicit (Galloway & Dunlop, 2007).

19 As elaborated in the book of R. Proterough and J. Pick in 2002.

The title of the previous European Cultural Programme (2007–2013) was changed to the "Creative Europe" Programme in 2014. One of the main goals of this new Creative Europe Programme should not be misunderstood: it is to enable the sectors to reach their economic potential, contributing to sustainable and inclusive growth, jobs, and social cohesion, among other goals.

According to David Throsby, there are even good strategic reasons for the arts and heritage sectors to be part of the definition of creative industries and to thereby also become a leverage for economic policy. He even calls the creative industries "the Trojan Horse" that will put the arts and the heritage sectors on the "international" policy agenda (Throsby, 2010).

1.6 European policy on entrepreneurship

EU and UN documents also set out arguments for why cultural and creative entrepreneurship is important to fulfil the potential of the creative industries. Although the EU believes strongly in this potential, all of the research that has been undertaken has come to the same conclusion: that one of the big barriers to the development of the full economic potential of the creative industries is the lack of entrepreneurial skills (The Entrepreneurial Dimension of the Cultural and Creative Industries, HKU, 2010, p. 139). Despite its importance, there is insufficient integration of entrepreneurship education into general curricula and arts education.

Through its Entrepreneurship 2020 Action Plan and its Communication on "Rethinking Education", the European Commission has emphasised the need to embed entrepreneurial learning in all sectors of education, including non-formal learning. One of the four strategic objectives of the Commission is "enhancing creativity and innovation, including entrepreneurship, at all levels of education and training" (EU Communication, "Rethinking Education: investing in skills for better socio-economic outcomes", November 2012). Both documents call on Member States to provide all young people with practical entrepreneurial experience before completing their compulsory education, highlighting the importance of *learning by doing* within education and training. This requires a way of teaching in which *experiential learning and project work* have a major role:

> *Teachers do not provide students with the answers, but help them to research and identify [the] right questions and find the best answers. To inspire their pupils and students, and to help them develop an enterprising attitude, teachers need a wide range of competences related to creativity and entrepreneurship; they require a school environment where creativity and risk-taking are encouraged, and mistakes are valued as a learning opportunity.*
>
> (European Commission, 2010)

Although the Entrepreneurship 2020 Action Plan of the EC presented some strong arguments in favour of making education more entrepreneurial, civil society criticised its main focus on the economic output of education and on the labour market. In particular, the arts education institutions asked the Commission to offer students time to learn and to experiment, to think outside the box, and to develop their own identity as an artist and creator:

> *European, national and regional policymakers should acknowledge the independent and different functions of (higher arts) education and the CCI sector should also be emphasised. Otherwise, Europe will lose its innovative potential and critical thinking, which is essential for an innovative creative sector. Educators and the CCI sector should share responsibility, invest in joint cooperation and overcome mutual prejudices.*
>
> (Rethinking Education, 2013)

In most countries, also the subsidised arts and heritage sector feels threatened by this economic approach by the EC and at other national and regional policy levels, as a response to the global financial crisis since 2008, which deeply affected society and the cultural sectors in particular. Many Western countries, like Italy, the Netherlands, and the UK decided to reduce subsidies for the arts and culture. As a consequence, new questions have arisen for the arts sector:

1. The question of the autonomy of the arts and how to respect this autonomy in a world dominated by motives strongly connected to the instrumental functioning of arts and culture.
2. The introduction of an evidence-based cultural policy (certainly in the UK and the Netherlands) that focuses on output and outcomes rather than on input and independent ideas (Snowball, 2008). The value of culture is being questioned.
3. The question of finance: most European countries (with the exception of the Nordic countries and Germany) have reduced subsidies for the cultural sector. Rather than relying primarily on government support, cultural organisations are now obliged to find other financial resources to survive. In the Netherlands, for example, arts organisations and museums must prove that they are entrepreneurial and can find income sources other than subsidies from the state or the region.

1.7 Entrepreneurship and cultural management education

The strong trend in recent years towards a more entrepreneurial-minded European welfare-state labour market undoubtedly has implications for cultural management education and training. Subsidised arts organisations need to adapt if they are to function in a completely new environment and within the perspective of the creative economy.

If we start from the notion that society in general, and the creative and cultural sectors in particular, are becoming more flexible, digital, and entrepreneurial, then the question arises: How can we prepare our students for this dynamic, but at the same time, uncertain modern work sphere? The traditional managerial approach remains very useful in terms of teaching people how to run art organisations, but in the competitive world of the creative industries, a technical "know-how" approach is limited to providing solutions on a more fundamental level, concerning cultural content, change management, and environmental turbulence. It could be argued that the impact of the current financial crisis on cultural management education needs to be addressed through a transition regarding content, process, and perspective. This would not merely require a new combination of existing experiences and courses, but a fundamentally new way of addressing the entrepreneurial organisation of art and culture. Jacobs and Kooyman (2015) distinguish a number of dilemmas that teachers in cultural management and entrepreneurship today are facing.

Dilemma 1: How do we teach risk-taking?

If a traditional art management education wants to respond to developments on a larger scale, a new entrepreneurial orientation needs to be developed.

Dilemma 2: How can we develop an intuitive mind?

Many studies show that entrepreneurs are rather more intuitive than rational thinkers (Kirby, 2004; Van Andel & Schramme, 2015). To cope with dynamic environments, it is important to have a well-developed sensitivity for the context in which one is working; something Jacobs and Kooyman like to call "context sensibility". This acquires a more holistic and syntactical way of looking at the world instead of a sequential reasoned and randomised method of exploration. Much psychological research shows that this human attribute is definitely something which can be developed through education: techniques like divergent thinking, ethnographic imagination, and hermeneutic interpretation could help to enhance this ability.

Dilemma 3: How do we prepare students for an uncertain world?

If we want students to be prepared for this uncertain world, one of the most important learning outcomes would have to be "self-awareness". This asks for personal leadership, the ability to put oneself on the line, being accountable, taking charge, and accepting failure as inherent to life and work.

Dilemma 4: How do we teach students to work together?

A "cultural entrepreneur" who enters the professional domain will be confronted with the fact that he needs to cooperate with others in small-scale, bottom-up networks. It is of the utmost importance to create a solid network in order to survive at all. The Cultural and Creative sectors highly depend on cooperation, project-based work, and interdisciplinarity, and demand a communal way of thinking.

Dilemma 5: How do we "preach" a sustainable attitude?

Cultural and Creative Entrepreneurs have to generate their individual earnings in a volatile market, with an abundance of cultural products around. Yet at the same time, they have to take care of creating a sustainable future. This means that they can't ignore moral and ethical questions, which arise in the global community. Therefore, it is important to discuss the social and ecological implications of entrepreneurship; not by preaching but by showing students that moral awareness is part of modern entrepreneurship (Jacobs & Kooyman, 2015).

1.8 Conclusion

From a historical perspective, cultural management as an education and research domain is quite young, and in Europe, it has primarily followed the main evolutions within society and changing political circumstances. While in the US, the first programmes had started already in the 1960s, in Europe, they only started in the 1980s, designed to assist the cultural sector to overcome the economic crisis and to become more resilient. Policymakers were also calling for more return on investment and sponsorship, with governments increasingly requiring evidence of planning and setting formal criteria for obtaining state subsidies. This led to the professionalisation of the cultural sector and a growing interest in cultural management education.

Since the 1990s, globalisation, migration, and digitisation, among other factors, have changed the conditions for arts and culture, with the old welfare models and funding systems undergoing dramatic change. The traditional borders between the artist and the audience have also been scrutinised, while established cultural institutions are struggling with underfunded budgets and a declining audience base. There has also been a shift in cultural policy, as the creative industries have been on the political agenda since the end of the 1990s, leading to more emphasis on an economic approach to arts and culture.

Future cultural managers working in European cultural organisations and projects will need the right knowledge, practical competences (craft), insights, and entrepreneurial skills – like intuition – to meet these challenges, as well as to navigate in somewhat new waters. If we consider management to be a practice that combines knowledge, craft, entrepreneurship, and insight, then, according to Verbergt, it is clear that it is the "insight" that distinguishes cultural managers from general managers. For Colbert and Evrard, cultural managers have also the experience to manage discontinuity. Artistic activities are, in this sense, prototypical. Their experiences in working with intermittent workers, dealing with dual management (artistic and business leadership) and specialising in what Evrard and Colbert refer to as "immateriality and patrimoniality" in finance and accounting, in a certain way make cultural managers excellent role models for general managers. The same could be said about cultural management educators: by exploring new methodologies and new ways of educating; by not only transferring knowledge but also including experience through internships and other practical-based courses by which students also get insight into the creative and cultural sectors; by their interdisciplinary approach, they are pioneers in the educational field and inspiring for other academic disciplines.

The development of information technology and digitally controlled communication has huge cultural implications, in changing cultural values, global civilisation, and the cultural landscape – creating cyberculture. Thus, it has already impacted not only arts management practices but above all, arts management education, as digital literacy will be one of the key arts/cultural management skills.

There is also a pressing need in the European cultural scene and in civil society to develop the capacity to provide the relevant analysis and create, develop, and change processes in cooperation with other players. Based on this evidence, we might argue that after the phase of the consolidation of cultural management education programmes in Europe, we are now entering a new phase: that of innovation (Hagoort, 2007). Innovation in education means looking for new ways that respond adequately to the new needs of the sector.

Arts/cultural management programmes that are implemented at university level have impacted the ways and methods of university teaching and learning, contributing towards the creation of different university "organisational cultures", cultures that promote innovation and creativity of both students and professors, making universities active cultural policy creators and agents of change within cultural and artistic practices. Practice-based research, policy analysis, or teaching focusing on problem-based and project-based learning, succeeded in connecting classrooms with burning issues of community cultural life (Dragićević-Šešić, 2008). At the same time, internships that situated students in cultural organisations and public institutions have further impacted universities with arts/cultural management and other practice-based cultural education to change their methods and teaching practices, and even to bring new modules in curricula that would be more responsive to demands of the job market (Bala, Gluhovic, Korsberg & Röttger, Eds. 2017).

This research has also shown the importance of ENCATC and other related European networks taking the role of platforms for innovation and exchange, offering insights into the processes of changing contemporary university culture, especially in the fields of arts, humanities, and social sciences. By showing how continuous innovation of the cultural and educational policies and practices (peer learning, research-based learning, project-based learning, practice-based learning, etc.) were reshaping the educational and cultural field, academics that are ENCATC members were and are emphasising the importance of knowledge creation and production (in both arts/cultural management and cultural policy) resulting in the positioning of cultural management as an academic discipline in its own rights.

1.9 Afterword – some additional and personal observations from Rod Fisher

When Annick Schramme concluded her fine analysis of the origins and development of creative and cultural management to mark the 25th Anniversary of ENCATC with the words "Interesting times ahead", I am sure she could not have imagined how prophetic her words would turn out to be! Of course, "interesting" in this context is a euphemism for how challenging and demanding recent years have been for the cultural and academic sectors. The COVID-19 pandemic in particular challenged the individual and collective resilience of those engaged in culture and learning, frequently forcing academia to re-examine the role of their institutions, the actions they take, and their relationship with students. In many respects, the pandemic diminished the student experience in some countries with the enforced emphasis on remote learning, the lack of live contact with tutors and fellow students for extended periods, and near empty campuses.

More recently, the Russian invasion of Ukraine has not only resulted in major economic impacts, it has also led to some uncomfortable experiences for some Russian students studying at higher education institutions in other countries. For example, they will have learnt the unvarnished truth that, in addition to the deaths of so many people, their Government's forces have deliberately targeted and destroyed many cultural buildings in Ukraine. Sadly, history teaches us that such actions are all too frequent when invaders are determined to eradicate a nation's cultural symbols and identity.

As we all know, the pandemic had serious impacts on the cultural sector in many European countries, with theatres, concert halls, museums, and cultural centres being forced to close for lengthy periods or reducing capacity in their venues, or restricting the numbers of visitors who want to see their exhibitions or collections. Perhaps the only positive outcome of the impact was that it accelerated the application of digital solutions and some imaginative ways to disseminate the work of cultural organisations. Arguably, the impact was especially devastating for the many freelance creators in the creative and cultural industries. Although a number of countries provided some assistance for their creative workforce, in others, there was minimal support, if any, as the focus of governments was primarily on the survival of cultural organisations. In the UK, a difficult situation was exacerbated by the self-inflicted decision to leave the EU. This came as a serious blow to the UK cultural sector in general and to freelance creatives in particular. Now they are no longer able to move freely in EU countries and find their work opportunities seriously reduced, especially short-notice engagements. As a consequence of Brexit and the pandemic, a significant number of freelance workers have abandoned careers in the creative and cultural industries.

Of course, crises in the cultural sector are not new. Throughout much of my 50+ year career in the arts, whether in local authorities, the Arts Council of Great Britain, or running my own research and information organisations (International Arts Bureau and then International Intelligence on Culture), the arts in the UK have often been in crisis. Usually, this was due to diminishing resources. Obviously, such difficulties have not been confined to the UK. One of the biggest crises I can recall was that which hit the cultural sector in those Central and Eastern European countries that shook off the yoke of the former USSR. Freedom of expression and freedom to travel came at a price. The realities of suddenly moving from a planned economy to a market one meant there were insufficient funds to meet the costs of running cultural institutions and paying staff and weak currencies provided a new barrier to travel. On a study visit to look at the cultural scene in Poland in 1989, I recall one theatre director joke that there was no unemployment in culture there, just unemployed people! His box office had a staff of 13, almost half of whom had no real job. Such employment security quickly vanished.

Inevitably, the pandemic crisis and Brexit have led to some in the UK questioning the value of running degree-level courses in the creative and cultural industries if the career prospects are limited. Of course, low salaries or irregular income can be part of the territory for those who seek to establish themselves in the field, but I hope that reduced employment opportunities may not deter some students from even trying. Moreover, with the focus of education policy in England increasingly on "core" subjects in the school curriculum, and with diminishing budgets over several years, the teaching of arts subjects is being seriously eroded. As I have said before, without opportunities to engage with, and be stimulated by, the arts, I cannot help wondering if there will be a sufficient number of aspiring creatives in the next generation.

Unfortunately, there are still too many people (at least in the UK) who consider degrees in culture, arts, and media to be "soft" options, of limited value compared to "serious" subjects such as economics, law, science, and medicine. Perhaps, for understandable reasons, we have devoted too much time talking amongst ourselves rather than to the wider community. ENCATC is full of imaginative people who may want to give some thought to that.

1.10 References

American Council for the Arts. (1983). *Survey of arts administration training 1982/83*. American Council for the Arts.

Andriopoulos, C. (2003). Six paradoxes in managing creativity: An embracing act. *Long Range Planning*, *36*(4), 375–388.

Bala, S., Gluhovic, M., Korsberg, H.., & Röttger, K. (Eds.). (2017). *International performance research pedagogies: Towards an unconditional discipline?* Palgrave Macmillan.

Bassand, M. (1993) *Culture and Regions of Europe*. Strasbourg: Council of Europe Publishing.

Baumol, W., & Bowen, W. (1966). *Performing arts: The economic dilemma*. Twentieth Century Fund.

Beckman, G. (2007). Adventuring' arts entrepreneurship curricula in higher education: An examination of present efforts, obstacles and best practices. *Journal of Arts Management, Law, and Society*, *37*(2), 87–112.

Bendixen, P. (2000). Skills and roles: Concepts of modern arts management. *International Journal of Arts Management*, *2*(3), 4–13.

Bloom, B. S. (Ed.). (1956). *Taxonomy of educational objectives: The classification of educational goals; Handbook I, Cognitive domain*. David McKay.

Brixy, U., Sternberg, R., & Stüber, H. (2008). *From potential to real entrepreneurship*. IAB Discussion Paper, Nuremberg.

Brixy, U., Sternberg, R., & Stuber, H. (2012). The Selectiveness of the Entrepreneurial Process. *Journal of Small Business Management*, *50*(1), 105–131.

Brkić, A. (2009). Teaching arts management: Where did we lose the core ideas? *The Journal of Arts Management, Law and Society*, *38*(4), 270–280. https://doi.org/10.3200/JAML.38.4.270-280

Busenitz, L. W., Page West III, G., Shepherd, D., Nelson, T., Chandler, G. N., & Zacharakis, A. (2011). Entrepreneurship research in emergence: Past trends and future directions. *Sage Journal of Management*, *29*(3).

Chiapello, E. (1998). *Artistes vs managers. Le management culturel face à la critique artiste*. Métailié.

De Block, A., & Heene, J. (1992). *Inleiding tot de algemene didactiek*. Standaard Educatieve Uitgeverij.

De Block, A., & Saveyn, J. (1985). *Didactische werkvormen en leerstrategieën*. Deurne: Plantyn.

DeFillippi, R., Grabher, G., & Jones, C. (2007). Introduction to paradoxes of creativity: managerial and organizational challenges in the cultural economy. *Journal of Organizational Behavior*, *28*(5), 511–521.

Deru, J., Dragićević-Šešić, M., & Goodacre, J. (Eds.). (2014). *Culture at the edges, celebrating 25 years of Trans-European training from Barcelona to Delphi*. Marcel Hicter.

Dietachmair, P., & Ilić, M. (Eds.) (2015). *Another Europe: 15 years of capacity building with cultural initiatives in the EU neighbourhood*. European Cultural Foundation.

Dimaggio, P. (1987). *Managers of the arts*. National Endowment for the Arts/ Seven Locks Press.

Dragićević-Šešić, M. (1978). Obrazovanje animatora kulture u Francuskoj. (Education of cultural animators in France). *Kultura*, *40*, 102–121. Institute for Cultural Development.

Dragićević-Šešić, M. (1997). Central Europe: cultural managers as mediators. In S. Esner & A. Palka (Eds.), *Challenges for cultural policy and management in Central and Eastern Europe*. Council of Europe & ENCATC.

Dragićević-Šešić, M. (2003). Survey on institutions and centers providing training for cultural development professionals in Eastern

Europe, Russian Federation, Central Asia and the Caucasus Region. In *Training in cultural policy and management, international directory of training centers*. UNESCO & ENCATC (www.encatc.org/media/409-training_in_cultural_policy_management_2003.pdf)

Dragićević-Šešić, M. (2008). New learning strategies: peer learning as the method in the teaching cultural cooperation in Europe. *TkH Journal for Performing Arts Theory*, *15*, 13–21.

Dragićević-Šešić, M. (2009). Educational programmes in strategic cultural management within the regional context. In *Cultural Policy and Management (KPY) yearbook*. Boekmanstudies; Istanbul Bilgi University Press.

Dragićević-Šešić, M. (2020). Contemporary arts in adaptable quality management: questioning entrepreneurialism as a panacea in Europe. In W. Byrnes & A. Brkić (Eds.), *The Routledge companion to arts management* (pp. 39–53). Routledge.

Dragićević-Šešić, M., & Mihaljinac, N. (2020). Cultural management training within cultural diplomacy agendas in the MENA region. In V. Durrer & R. Henze (Eds.), *Managing culture: Reflecting on exchange in global times* (pp. 205–232). Palgrave Macmillan.

Dubois, V. (2013). *Culture as a vocation: Sociology of career choices in cultural management*. Routledge.

Ebewo, P., & Sirayi, M. (2009). The concept of arts/cultural management: A critical reflection. *The Journal of Arts Management, Law and Society*, *38*(4), 281–295. https://doi.org/10.3200/JAML.38.4.281-295

European Commission (2010). *Unlocking the Potential of Cultural and Creative Industries: Green Paper*. Publications Office of the European Union.

EUEuropean Task Force on Culture and Development. (1997). *In from the margins. A contribution to the debate on culture and development in Europe*. Council of Europe.

Evrard, Y., & Colbert, F. (2000). Arts management: A new discipline entering the millennium. *International Journal of Arts Management*, 2(2), 4–13.

Fillis, I. (2006). Art for art's sake or art for business sake: An exploration of artistic product orientation. *The Marketing Review*, *6*, 29–40.

Fisher, R., & Karpodini-Dimitriadi, E. (Eds.) (2007). *Training in transnational cultural cooperation projects*. Reflections and Challenges on Validation and Certification. VANIA Project.

Fisher, R., & Mitchell, R. (1992). *Professional managers for the arts and culture? Training of cultural administrators and arts managers in Europe*. The Arts Council of Finland, Council of Europe (Council for Cultural Co-operation) CIRCLE. Helsinki University Press.

Galloway, S., & Dunlop, S. (2007). A critique of definitions of the cultural and creative industries in public policy. *International Journal of Cultural Policy*, *13*(1). Taylor & Francis.

Gielen, P., Elkhuizen, S., Van Den Hoogen, Q., Lijster, Th., & Otte, H. (2014). *De waarde van cultuur* (187 p.). Onderzoeksopdracht (onderzoekscentrum Arts in Society. Rijksuniversiteit Groningen), Socius.

Grbac, Ž. (1989). *Kultura i društvo* (*Culture and society*). Školska knjiga.

Hagoort, G. (2005). *Art management: Entrepreneurial style* (3rd ed., 296 p.). Eburon Publishers.

Hagoort, G. (2007). Cultureel ondernemerschap. Over het onderzoek naar de vrijheid van kunst maken en de vrijheid van ondernemen. *Oratie 6 juni 2007* (69 p.). Faculteit der Kunsten – vakgebied Kunst en economie, Universiteit Utrecht/Faculteit Kunst en Economie-Lectoraat Kunst en Economie, Hogeschool voor de Kunsten Utrecht.

Hagoort, G. (2010). *The entrepreneurial dimension of the cultural and creative industries*. Hogeschool voor de Kunsten.

Hammet, M. (1989). The evolution of arts management studies. *Journal of Arts Policy and Management*, *3*(3). City University.

Hauenstein, A. D. (1998). *A conceptual framework for educational objectives: A holistic approach to traditional taxonomies*. University Press of America.

Hutter, M., & Throsby, D. (Eds.). (2008). *Beyond price. Value in culture, economics and the arts*' (315 p.). Cambridge University Press.

Jacobs, R., & Kooyman, R. (2015). The entrepreneurial ant. Rethinking arts management education. In O. Kuhle, A. Schramme, & R. Kooyman (Eds.), *Creating cultural capital. Cultural entrepreneurship in theory, pedagogy and practice*. Eburon, University of Chicago Press.

Janetski, B. K. (2007). *Managing creative environments: The case of creative managers in regional theatre groups*. University of Minnesota.

Johansson, T., & Luonila, M. (Eds.). (2017). *Making sense of arts management, research cases and practices: 20 years of arts management education in Finland, Sibelius Academy Publications no*' (Vol. 11, pp. 7–8). Sibelius Academy of the University of the Arts Helsinki.

Kirby, D. (2004) Entrepreneurship education: can business schools meet the challenge? *Education + Training*, *46*(8/9), 510–519.

Kirchberg, V., & Zembylas, T. (2010). Arts Management: A Sociological Inquiry. *The Journal of Arts Management Law and Society*, (1), 1–5.

Klamer, A. (1996). *The value of culture. On the relationship between economics and arts* (243 p.). Amsterdam University Press, .

Kolsteeg, J. (2014). *Shifting gear. The daily deliberation between arts and economics in cultural and creative organisations in Utrecht, 2010–2012* (209 p.). Eburon Publishers.

Kotler, P., & Scheff, J. (1997). *Standing room only: Strategies for marketing the performing arts*. Harvard Business School Press.

Kuesters, I. (2010). Arts managers as liaisons between finance and arts: A qualitative study inspired by the theory of functional differentiation. *The Journal of Arts Management, Law, and Society*, *40*, 43–57. https://doi.org/10.1080/10632921003603976

Kuhle, O., Schramme, A., & Kooyman, R. (Eds.). (2015). *Creating cultural capital. Cultural entrepreneurship in theory, pedagogy and practice*. Eburon Delft, University of Chicago Press.

Lampel, J., Lant, Th., & Shamsie, J. (2000). Balancing act: Learning from organizing practices in cultural industries. *Organization Science*, *11*(3), 263–269.

Mandel, B. (2015). *Arts/cultural management in international contexts. Results of a research on the views of arts/cultural managers around the world regarding their profession, working conditions, current challenges, required competencies, and training opportunities*. Hildesheim University/Olms Verlag Hildesheim 2017.

Noordman, Th. B. J. (1993). *Op zoek naar de fundamenten van een Kunstmanagementtheorie.* In Bevers, T.; Van Den Braembussche, A.; Langenberg B. J. (Red.). *De Kunstwereld. Produktie, distributie, en receptie in de wereld van kunst en cultuur* (385 p.). Rotterdam: Erasmus Universiteit.
Noordman, Th. B. J. (2010). *10e Carl Birnielezing. Afscheidscollege Dirk Noordman op 21 januari 2010* (16 p.). Erasmus Universiteit.
Parker, S. C. (2009). *The economics of Entrepreneurship.* Cambridge University Press.
Pick, J. (1980). *Arts administration.* E. & F. N. Spon.
Pratt, A. C. (2013). The Cultural and Creative Industries: New Engines for the City? *Culture: City*, 36–42.
Proterough, R., & Pick, J. (2002). *Managing Britannia.* Edgeways.
Rethinking Education. Empowering individuals with the Appropriate Educational Tools, Skills and Competencies, for their Active Cultural, Political and Economic Participation in Society, Europe and beyond. (2013, December). *A compilation of essays.* Published by Access to Culture. Platform in the context of the structured dialogue with Member States and the European Commission, Brussels, House for Culture.
Snowball, J. D. (2008). *Measuring the value of culture. Methods and examples in cultural economics* (230 p.). Springer Verlag.
Şuteu, C. (2006). *Another brick in the wall: A critical review of cultural management education in Europe.* Boekmanstudies.
Throsby, D. (2010). *The economics of cultural policy.* Cambridge University Press.
UK Department for Culture, Media and Sport (DCMS). (1998). Creative Industries Mapping Document, 1998. http://www.creativitycultureeducation.org/creative-industries-mapping-document-1998
Van Andel, W., & Schramme, A. (2015). Exploring entrepreneurial actions of creative entrepreneurs and its consequences for entrepreneurship education. In O. Kuhle, A. Schramme, & R. Kooyman (Eds.), *Creating cultural capital: cultural entrepreneurship in theory, pedagogy and practice: pioneering minds worldwide* (p. 25). Eburon, University of Chicago Press.
Varela, X. (2013). Core consensus, strategic variations: Mapping arts management graduate education in the United States. *The Journal of Arts Management, Law and Society, 43*(4), 74–87.
Verbergt, B., & De Bruyne, L. (2015). Companions, not general managers. In O. Kuhle, A. Schramme, & R. Kooyman (Eds.), *Creating cultural capital: cultural entrepreneurship in theory, pedagogy and practice: pioneering minds worldwide* (pp. 151–164). Eburon, University of Chicago Press.
Watt, D., & Welton, R. (1990). *Training, national arts & media strategy discussion document 13.* Arts Council of Great Britain.
Wesner, S., & Palka, A. (Eds.) (1997). *Challenges for Cultural Policy and Management in Central and Eastern Europe.* Council of Europe, ENCATC.
Whitley, R. (1989). On the nature of managerial tasks: Their distinguishing characteristics and organisation. *Journal of Management Studies, 26*(3), 209–225.
Whitley, R. (1995). Academic knowledge and work jurisdiction in management. *Organization Science, 16*(1), 81–105.
Wiesand, A. (2002, February). Comparative cultural policy research in Europe: A change of paradigm. *Canadian Journal of Communication, 27*(2).
World Commission on Culture and Development. (1995). *Our creative diversity.* UNESCO.

2 Unravelling the palimpsest of transnational networks in cultural and creative sectors

Reflections on networks, politics, and their usages

Carlotta Scioldo

"The history of international cultural networking is still to be written. One day it might be valued as important knowledge, because it certainly influences the conception of arts and culture", writes Hugo De Greef, pioneering culture entrepreneur and founder of the Kaaitheater Brussels, in the landmark publication "Give, get or get off! Challenges of cultural networking today" (De Greef, 2008). De Greef's observations emphasize that the history of networks has had a significant influence on the conception of arts and culture, and more broadly, has played a key role in shaping European cultural governance by crossing boundaries and overcoming differences. When the European Festival Association was founded in 1952, under the initiative of Swiss intellectual Denis de Rougemont, it was able to bridge the Iron Curtain that had divided Eastern and Western Europe. Festivals from former communist countries could join the network, strengthening relationships and exchanging information, via yearly meetings of festival directors. During a period of significant political changes, two landmark events led to the creation of diverse long-lasting transnational networks, among them is the European Network of Cultural Administration Training Centres (ENCATC). Starting as an informal meeting, ENCATC was institutionalised with the aim of promoting mobility, cooperation, and communication, shortly after the fall of the Iron Curtain. The first event was a meeting in Hamburg in 1987 aimed at forming an informal network by bringing together art schools, universities, and training centers for arts management courses. The second event was a conference in Barcelona in 1990, supported by Eduard Delgado from the Council of Europe, which highlighted the importance of cultural management education. ENCATC was established after the Council of Europe took action during a 1992 meeting in Warsaw to formally address the need for an educational and training program for cultural workers. ENCATC's first undertaking

DOI: 10.4324/9781003594413-2

was to hold summer schools that analysed and evaluated cultural policies and management issues on a comparative European level (ENCATC, 2017, p. 28).

Learning from the role of cultural networking in the past helps us imagine the transnational impact of cultural ecosystems in the future. Thus, it remains a crucial question today to explore how networks have been discursively inscribed, erased, and rewritten over time, and to inquire: *what are networks for, and who does what and how?* These simple questions entail complex factors, as networks are structures continuously evolving, and their evolution constantly (re)frames their significance.

European networks have grown considerably over the last three decades, driven by EU cultural policy and its respective funding programmes – namely Kaleidoscope, Culture 2000, and Creative Europe – in support of cultural cross-border cooperation. Networks have not only been instrumental to the key developments in the EU cultural agenda and to the evolution of its cultural and creative diverse ecosystems, but they have also contributed to shifts in EU values, frameworks, and institutional governance.

Such cultural networks are discursively linked to the question of *participation* and *governance, and more widely to the construction of a public sphere.* Within the EU, their founding purposes have always been to enhance greater awareness of culture and arts in society within the international context, by promoting co-productions or lobbying for cultural policy changes (EFA, 2006). After first emerging as informal gatherings among cultural practitioners in the late 1980s, such networks have been increasingly institutionalised through the EU since the 2000s, primarily through grant opportunities. Within the framework of the EU's cultural policy and its subsidiarity principle, according to which cultural competencies should remain under the authority of Member States, networks have been considered an ideal tool to overcome deficits that have resulted from the subsidiary principle. Cultural practitioners have reported the emergence of networks as a response to the competencies and fields of action – or lack thereof – characterising the EU's cultural policy. Practitioners expressed this reasoning as follows:

> *this idea of subsidiarity . . . , for which the European Commission said: we are not going to fund creation because according to subsidiarity, this is a task of the Member States. So, what we can do is fund everything else***:** *the networking, the translation, the mobility, all of the new keywords that one sees in the new documents . . . anything that they could define that was not going to be something that the member states would have to claim that was their competence only.*
>
> (Interview)[1]

1 The interviews were conducted with professionals working in the executive offices of Creative Europe granted Networks and/or who were members of its Board of Directors as part of the

Although networks' hybrid position between cultural policy and the independent cultural sector has been a focal point of their evolution, academic researchers have struggled to conceptualise their role in this multilevel perspective. This lack of research about transnational networks in the CCS ultimately fails to provide interpretative frameworks to correctly analyse this phenomenon and thus hinders a realisation of the full potential for their further evolution.

This chapter proposes to analyse networks' evolution using public policy awareness – as a perspective complementing that of cultural management – in order to reveal the underpinning political implications of mainstreaming these practices within the EU context. This would allow us to better situate their actions in the political debate.

It is in fact by considering these structures as both having a top-down coordinative function and serving as a bottom-up civil society initiative that it becomes possible to depict networks as multidimensional and multi-interest platforms, and to analyse their influential role in shaping both policies and sectoral outcomes.

To address this analytical gap, this chapter offers insights into the discourse and concepts from both officials and practitioners, drawing on perspectives from various disciplines to enrich the debate on the multilevel positioning of networks and the politics that underpin them. This allows us to better conceptualise their multidimensional relevance: towards policy on various levels (EU, national, and sub-national), the cultural sector, and the network's members, to then ultimately shed light on how these aggregated actors function as the backbone of European cultural governance.

To begin such a reflection, it is essential to recognise that policy instruments – and networks can be partially considered as such here – are not neutral, but political choices (Lascoumes, 2003 in Bruno et al., 2006). Hence processes such as learning, socialisation, and adaptation happen among diverse institutional and non-governmental actors in the EU, resulting in the creation of specific politics.

Furthermore, the evolution of networks has been closely tied to the EU framework, funding schemes, and the creation of a European public sphere, which is the result of discursive negotiations between various institutional and civic actors (see also Lähdesmäki et al., 2019). As a result, an interdisciplinary approach, drawing from comparative politics and public policy, as well as cultural policy studies, is necessary to analyse these instruments. Analytical frameworks such as those presented by Dossi (2012), Jacquot and Woll (2003, 2004, 2010), Radaelli (2000, 2004, 2008), and Schmidt (2000, 2002,

research Ph.D. thesis titled "Transnational Networks between European Governance and local changes in the Cultural and creative sector; if not for harmonizing policies, then what?" in the period 2021–2022. The dissertation was defended at the Interuniversity Department of Regional and Urban Studies and Planning – University of Turin and Polytechnic – on 7 November 2022.

2018) offer a bottom-up sensitivity to Europeanisation processes and a deep understanding of institutional governance architecture, while emphasising the role of political actors – in our case, cultural practitioners – as protagonists of transformative political changes. Embracing this interpretative lens supports in depitcing the development of cultural networking as a result of the influences of EU values and governance arrangements.

Finally, to capture the complexity of the textual and discursive layers in which EU-granted networks are embedded, the format of this chapter/dossier follows the template of the Creative Europe Programme granting application, following the criteria assessed: *Relevance, Quality of Content and Activities; Communication and Dissemination; Quality of the European Network (EACEA 39/2016).* This chapter uses these same award criteria as starting questions and conceptual guidelines to systematise academic, grey literary sources and empirical materials. Employing such a format provides a platform for different narratives to merge and renew debates between policy, networks, and practitioners with the aim to uncover a multi-layered understanding of cultural networks. The purpose here is to acknowledge their intricate governance system and reveal the overlapping of these structures – grassroots organisations and soft policy mechanisms – through their respective narratives.

Ultimately, this text serves as a reminder that networks are part of a broader governance architecture, and that their effectiveness greatly depends on a comprehensive understanding of their multidimensional structures.

2.1 Relevance

The *Relevance* criterion of the Creative Europe Programme application assesses: "How relevant is the project's strategy to implement one or more of the following priorities? . . . How relevant is the project to the needs of the targeted sector(s)?" (EACEA 39/2016, p. 15).

In 1996, MEP Roy Perry commented on the potential significance of networking, noting that there would be more compelling arguments to be made to politicians for network's value if concrete statistics were available to demonstrate its impact and effectiveness. Perry argued that such statistics should be solidly informed by an understanding of network actions ("What do networks do?"), impacts ("What are the results?"), and effectiveness ("Where is the proof?") (IETM, 2001, p. 8). This chapter proposes a complementary perspective, suggesting that the relevance of networks is best understood in the context of the EU's cultural governance arrangement, where these structures serve both as tools of a new model of governance and as an aggregate of resources and interests from the cultural sector. How networks are perceived, named, and interpreted is thus strongly influenced by this layered understanding.

Cultural networking is the label most often employed by transnational networks operating in the cultural and creative sectors to denote their own activities, according to several milestone sources (IETM, 2001; CoE, 2002; EFA, 2007; CAE, 2016; Kooperativa, 2022). While this label reflects a bottom-up sensitivity on the subject and emphasises the importance of networking, it also narrows our understanding of these organisations and their wider implications in practices and activities, as explained below. In reality, transnational networks are characterised by their multilevel structure that depends on their controversial origins. By the late 1980s, networks were established informally by cultural professionals as a means for exchanging practices and strengthening international collaboration. Then, with the encouragement of the EU Council of Ministries to explore "with Member States the possibility available to networks to play a part in cultural action" with the purpose of an "active participation by cultural organisations in cooperation at the European level" (CoE, 2002, p. 41), these structures were gradually integrated into the European Union infrastructure and institutionalised through EU programmes and funding initiatives in the early 2000s.

This evolution illustrates a complex dynamic, in which the European Commission and the Council of Europe acted as "purposeful opportunists" (Cram, 1993, 1997, 2011) in policy sectors without formal competencies, such as the cultural sector, creating an ad hoc transnational "community" through network structures and other programmes with the aim to legitimise EU actions. These actions pursuing the creation of a structural dialogue with the cultural sector proved to be crucial to enhance mobility, cooperation, and communication (CoE, 2000, p. 3 in ENCATC, 2017, p. 26), while at the same time have strengthened the European dimension of the activities and involved actors. Furthermore, networks embedded the shift of the EU architecture into an increasingly evolving network governance with the intent of disseminating EU values across levels. In conformity with this latter understanding, scholars have argued that European institutions have sought to promote European citizenship through social engineering processes via diverse funding schemes for cultural projects and soft policy mechanisms, including policy and civil society network organisations (Shore, 2002; Kaiser, 2015; Lähdesmäki, 2016; Lähdesmäki et al., 2019).

By contrast, a bottom-up sensitivity reveals that these networks emerged in the late 1980s as informal gatherings among cultural professionals with the goal of centralising sector interests, serving as exchange and networking platforms, and advocating for representation with various institutional and para-institutional actors, including European institutions. Developed parallel to the consolidation of the civil society sector and the independent cultural scene, networks have become essential for the sustainability of the independent cultural sector in various contexts, particularly in Southeastern European regions (Kooperativa, 2022, p. 10).

In the context of the fall of the Iron Curtain, networking has played a fundamental role as a response to the necessity to "bring back international cultural dialogue" as a counter to the isolation, as Andrè Plesu – former Minister of Culture and Romanian dissident – stated (CoE, 2002, p. 39). In line with this, scholars have emphasised the significant role of civil society organisations in ensuring that public interests are met within institutional contexts, by partly safeguarding "the trust of the citizens in their society and its institutions" (Dragicevic Sesic & Dragojevic, 2006 in T. Pureber (Ed.), 2022, 5). In other words, cultural practitioners succeeded in acquiring a representational and political stance through the emergence and consolidation of networks, resulting in their position as change-makers in multilevel governance. Aligned with this latter perspective, a bottom-up sensitivity to Europeanisation studies (Jacquot & Woll, 2003, 2004, 2010), which evolved emphasising individual actions (see micro-foundation of personal motivations) and their role in the transformations of the EU political system, is beneficial in analysing this phenomenon. The term "usage" (as per Jacquot & Woll, 2003, 2004) was offered as a conceptual lens for cognitive and strategic dynamics in the study of European transformations (Jacquot & Woll, 2010), making political and civil society actors the protagonists of change within the political arrangement. This perspective reveals that the EU and its programmes' influence is not only derived from "EU norms per se" but rather from "informal interactions involving transnational mutual learning" (Malandrino, 2020, p. 547). As such, the relationship with the EU is considered as "practices and political interactions occurring back and forth between the European and the national, local, sectoral, institutional" (Jacquot & Woll, 2003, p. 4), and non-governmental level. This dynamic creates "a context of reciprocal influence" (ibid.), rather than a unidirectional adaptational pressure on institutional structures, thus emphasising the role of individual actions. It is in this frame that networks are positioned.

Overall, to effectively assess the relevance of a network in addressing [policy] priorities, it is essential to recognise both the top-down and bottom-up dimensions at play. A more comprehensive understanding allows for a clearer positioning of networks within multi-directional influences, linking them to issues such as participation, ownership, and governance, as well as the broader context of shaping an European public sphere. In this sphere, the balance between consensus and dissensus is key to fostering dynamic democratic engagement. It is by examining both the power dynamics within networks and their potential impact on EU governance arrangements that is possible to gain a deeper awareness of networks and their implications for policy, academic, and cultural communities. Further, clarifying the analytical perspective adopted in observing networks – whether this be *from the top, from the bottom, or inside-out* – shed light on the underlying meaning of the terms such as "network", "cultural network", "cultural networking", or "transnational network in the cultural and creative sector" and uncover their usage.

2.2 Quality of content and activities

In the Creative Europe Programme granting application, the following questions are regarding *Quality of content and activities*: "How clear and feasible is the architecture of the project (relation between objectives, activities, results)? . . . How relevant are the activities to the objectives of the project and the needs of the target group?" (EACEA 39/2016, p. 16).

To promote mobility, cooperation, and communication (CoE, 2000: 3 in ENCATC, 2017, p. 26), cultural and interdisciplinary networks have increased their range of activities over time, for a wider plethora of stakeholders. Grey literature has identified four main areas of expertise that these networks have developed: (1) service and information, (2) research and knowledge, (3) training and education, and (4) networking (CoE, 2002; EFA, 2007; CAE, 2016; IFACCA, 2016). However, to truly understand the impact of these networks, it is important to empirically recognise "what networks do" to then clarify "what are the results" (IETM, 2001). Outreach and advocacy, working groups, thematic newsletters, communication campaigns, joint policy papers, productions, projects, peer-to-peer knowledge exchange, and symposia (CAE, 2016; Kooperativa, 2022), to name just a few, are some of the means that a network put in place to reach its strategic long-term objectives. Throughout these activities, networks facilitate capacity-building and increase awareness within the sector they represent, in line with their vision, mission, and strategic development. In more general terms, the activities are designed to represent the *mutual values* and principles at the core of the networks' mission and are intended to enhance the *mutual empowerment* of the membership (Pureber, 2022, pp. 18–19).

The literature on networks (Busse, 2008; Giest & Howlett, 2013; Gerristen, 2016; Jacobsson, 2004) has thus far emphasised the *horizontal mechanism – deep networking* – at the core of these structures and working modes. This approach describes how processual dynamics such as "mutual identification, loyalty shifts, actor socialisation and internalisation of norms, [and] learning processes" (Haas, 1992) contribute to the emergence of epistemic communities that are built upon common interests, purposes, and values, ultimately resulting in "common cognitive frames" (Jacobsson, 2004, p. 1). But what distinguishes these new modes of governance is the engagement of actors ranging from grassroots organisations to institutional entities in a vertical multilevel scenario. It is only by acknowledging both the horizontal and vertical dimensions of networks, that we can ensure their proper functioning and effective use as participative devices. By relying on the strength of horizontal processes, vertical changes can be achieved, and vice versa. It is in line with such an understanding that the activities can be therefore considered as the outcomes of multi-directional processes of influence. The acknowledgement of this multi-directional influence is crucial when referring to network effectiveness.

The search for "the effects of networking" (IETM, 2001) is a critical long-lasting question, which different studies have sought to address since the 2000s. The attempt initially was to move beyond the anecdotal principle underpinning networkers' practices and to develop additional valid proof of networking's effects to bring more evidence of the networking movement as arguments for their benefits in advocating to public authorities. In this search, what initially emerged as remarkable was recognising the invaluable feature of networks as "fertile terrain for the growth of ideas and serving as an incubator of innovation" (IETM, 2001, p. 23) – that is, precisely their horizontal *deep networking*. Their function as catalysers and incubators has been recognised many times, but their potential and impact extend far beyond this function. To properly respond to the question of *how relevant the activities to the [network] objectives [are]*, it is once again advantageous to recognise networks' multilevel dimension and thereby capture their effectiveness on diverse levels, meaning towards policy (EU, national, and sub-national), the transnational cultural sector, and members' local context.

2.3 Communication and dissemination

The *Communication and dissemination* criterion of the Creative Europe Programme application assesses: "How clear and appropriate is the strategy to communicate the activities (target groups, tools, channels, media, impact, and timeline)? How clear and appropriate is the strategy to disseminate as widely as possible the experience and knowledge acquired (i) through the project and/or (ii) through other (Creative Europe-funded) projects during and beyond the duration of the project?" (EACEA 39/2016, p. 16).

Patterns of communication, benchmarking, policy learning, and promotion of new policy paradigms are some of the fundamental characteristics of soft and new modes of governance (Börzel & Risse, 2000 in Dossi, 2012).

When studying EU cultural policy and its soft mechanisms – as per networks – it is fundamental to acknowledge the feature of the policy as highly ideational, and thus as implying an emphasis on the creation and dissemination of discourse across various levels. Dealing with discourse and ideas is particularly significant for a coordinative and non-binding policy sector that takes shape primarily through the discursive interaction of institutional and non-institutional actors in a governance arrangement. In this regard, the discursive power of ideas generated and propagated within the institutional setting (Schmitt, 2015, p. 106) takes on central importance for policy analysis and policy change.

According to scholars who draw from discursive turns in studying the domestic impact of Europe (Schmidt & Radaelli, 2004; Lombardo & Forest, 2013), discourse is considered both as policy ideas and as "the interactive process of formulation and communication that serve to generate and disseminate those policy ideas" (Schmidt, 2002). Discourse is therefore considered as a process through which ideas such as policies, programmes, and philosophies are conveyed through actor interactions, implying consideration of both individual actions and the underlying structural arrangement from which they emerge as discursively intertwined. In the EU's sui generis multilevel system, both coordinative (occurring among policy actors) and communicative discourse (open towards the public sphere) are simultaneously at play (ibid.), ensuring an interactive process of discussion between policymakers and citizens. This kind of dynamic maintains a balance between stability and change within the institutional setting, thus ensuring its legitimacy and democratic nature.

Such an understanding of discourse (Schmidt, 2002, 2018; Schmidt & Radaelli, 2004) allows us to unpack not only the key role of networks in ensuring the communicative dimension of discourse in the EU framework – meaning the outreach towards the public sphere – but also the politics of the multilevel actors involved in this discursive interaction. This analytical lens understands networks as structural enablers of an ongoing discursive, interactive process that contributes to disseminating EU values across levels. Such an understanding is in line with scholars (Sassatelli, 2010; Kaiser, 2015; Lähdesmäki et al., 2021) who have described EU cultural policy as a mode to promote Europeanisation through policies and programmes centred around specific ideas and discourses, which are then transmitted across levels through actions and projects. While networks transmit discourse across levels, they also upscale cultural practices and concerns from the field, shaping them through governance mechanisms and transnational influence. In this case, the emphasis on actor ideas and discourse as an engine of the political process (Schmidt, 2018) highlights the roles that cultural professionals increasingly assumed once they become beneficiaries of EU grant schemes. While cultural professionals ensure the representation of cultural sectors and civil society values, they do in fact also discursively and cognitively devise a European public sphere, or, as one practitioner well explained, contribute to building "a European cultural space" (see below) which, I am arguing here, also has symbolic dimensions.

> *The model of co-producing, co-creating, co-showing [sic] in whatever way it is, whether it's a visual art, exhibition, or choir goes hand in hand with the* ***making of the European Cultural Space*** *that goes hand in hand with the European Commission, the European Union, and its policies.*
>
> (Interview)

By examining patterns of communication, dissemination, and benchmarking, it becomes possible to reveal the potential of networks to support sectors' interests, practices, and discourse. At the same time, this process enables the co-creation of the public sphere by fostering actors' discursive interaction, or, more simply, by fueling public debate.

2.4 Quality of the European network

The criterion "Quality of the European Network" pertains to the network's representativeness, specifically the number and types of its members (EACEA 39/2016, 6).

Community-based approaches, participatory modes of governance, and new business models are long-standing key concepts in the EU cultural landscape and discourse. Networks originally arose as a means of widening participation in policymaking, but it (Kern & Bulkeley, 2009) has pointed out that these structures can also have the unintended consequence of undermining democratic legitimacy in decision-making processes. This is due to the observed tendency of bottom-up and self-governance structures to result in closed elite circles in policymaking. Broadly speaking, if "governance is understood as an analytical concept describing political processes of negotiation and steering" (see also Meckling, 2004, p. 51 in Schmitt, 2009, p. 22), then cultural governance is not defined as being completely different from any other sectorial field of governance, since it is conceived as "the reconstruction of politico-social steering of institutions" (Meckling, 2004, p. 30 in Schmitt, 2009, p. 22).

In network structures, governance encompasses the mechanisms established to guarantee democratic participation and broad representation among members. Together with the executive office, these devices ensure the diversity and representativeness that, guarantee network accountability. In the evolution of networks from self-governance mechanisms to a rather centralised hub of competence and knowledge, in which information and skills – financial, political, administrative, and sectorial – are aggregated and tasks are handled on a day-to-day basis, the executive office is defined as a "managerial body to which member actors delegate the organisational responsibilities of facilitating the network-wide development of new approaches and strategies for tackling complex policy problems" (Provan & Milward, 2001). The institutionalization of networks went in hand with establishing executive offices with ad hoc governance mechanisms to increase network efficiency. However, increased centralisation has raised the issue of membership participation, thus calling for membership accountability and representation. Conclusively, as a response to the question of *how representative a network is of the sector(s) in which it operates*, new tendencies arose, such as the widening, in size and type, of the membership and decentralisation strategies of office competencies. These tactics have experimented in countering such centralised knowledge hubs, with the purpose of maintaining networks' legitimacy and accountability over time while keeping their relevance up-to-date.

2.5 Appendix

As this article dossier demonstrates, cultural networks operate as a crucial link between the policy and cultural sectors, institutional and experimental discourses, and formal and informal tactics. By facilitating spaces that foster *appropriation, re-appropriation, engagement*, and the *disengagement* of diverse actors' narratives and interests, these networks play a critical role in the complex tapestry of instruments, policy initiatives, and coalitions that make up EU cultural policy. In effect, they serve as connective tissue, linking the yet-to-be-associated dots and catalysing social, cultural, and discursive transformations at various levels.

Cultural policies are non-binding and highly ideational at the EU level, and fragmented at the national, sub-national, and lower levels. It is therefore a challenge to identify how organisational structures of networks possessing critical, and thus tactical, functions operate in the cultural sector, because – unlike in other policy areas – harmonisation or policy convergence cannot be expected in this field. A broader question thus arises: *what, then, are networks used for?*

To answer this question, it is important to trace the origin of these networks back to the late 1980s when cultural professionals first convened informally. These structures also arise as embedded in ideational principles linked to the Lisbon Strategy (Borrás & Radaelli, 2011), which has the purpose of enhancing intense knowledge production and disseminating EU discourse, ideas, and values across different levels (Littoz-Monnet, 2012; Mattocks, 2018). These tactical bodies have arisen from EU values and principles and have been instrumental in promoting inclusivity and diversity in policy-making processes, thereby ensuring the creation of a European public sphere:

> *Let me start once again with the prehistory, . . . in those years we [the networks] were fighting with the DG [EAC], . . . we [the networks] said we are doing your [DG EAC] job: we read all of the policy papers at that time, which were very few. And we [the networks] said, we are doing what you [DG EAC] are supposed to be doing: we are making the European cultural space.*
>
> (Interview)

In this sense, their function and actions can be acknowledged as the backbone of European cultural governance.

To truly understand how networks evolved in such a complex environment as the EU governance arrangement, however, it is necessary to combine both structural and actor perspectives and examine the role of political actors – cultural actors, in our case – as fundamental in enabling transformative changes. It is by adopting a simultaneous *top-down* and *bottom-up* sensitivity to public and cultural policy studies, and by emphasising on the *role of political actors* that we can gain a deeper understanding of the interconnectedness of discourse and governance, and better untangle their mutual influences. Such understanding makes it possible to unpack the potential of networks in their multilevel and multifunctional dimension.

Hence to properly respond to the questions of *how relevant a network is in addressing the [policy] priorities, how relevant the activities [are] to the [network] objectives, how clear and appropriate the strategy [is] to . . . the knowledge acquired [within the network]* and *how representative a network is of the sector(s) (EACEA 39/2016)*, it is crucial to follow an inside-out approach encompassing the different voices at play. This allows networks to be positioned more clearly among multi-directional influences and therefore as discursively linked with the question of *participation, ownership*, and *governance*. In conclusion, in the ongoing effort to clarify the term "network", its practices, and its usages, public policy awareness – as complementary to the cultural management perspective – has done well to acknowledge the horizontal and vertical dimensions, the top-down and bottom-up influences simultaneously at play in network structures. Elucidating this multi-directional influence is key to understand network effectiveness. Following this approach, a research agenda encompassing the diverse, but intertwined, units of analysis (transnational network, membership, and EU governance) would need to be further explored throughout the course of their interactions.

We can conclude by saying that these bodies are "way[s] of organizing rather than organisation[s]" (CoE, 2001, p. 36) that emerged from the "desire to co-operate" (CoE, 2001, p. 31) and from "enormous energy and thirst for change" (CoE, 2001, p. 62), and that their potential as tools of building an ideational spatiality of Europe, through infrastructural resources, practices, and ideas, remains to be further explored. They are dynamic entities that thrive on the involvement of individuals and groups, making them adaptable and resilient to challenges throughout their life cycle. And as long as their purpose remains pressing, their relevance for policy, for the cultural sector in which they operate, and for network members will remain vibrant. However, as Anne Bieler has reminded us: "Networks can go out like a constellation of stars, but one must be sure that the disappearance is a natural one."

Declaration of interest statement

No potential conflict of interest was reported by the author(s).

The interviews were conducted with professionals working in the executive offices of Creative Europe granted Networks and/or who were members of its Board of Directors as part of the research Ph.D. thesis titled "Transnational Networks between European Governance and local changes in the Cultural and Creative sector; if not for harmonizing policies, then what?" in the period 2021–2022. The dissertation was defended at the Interuniversity Department of Regional and Urban Studies and Planning – University of Turin and Polytechnic – on 7 November 2022.

2.6 References

Bieler, Anne. (1997). *The Role of Cultural Networks in European Cultural Policy*. Council of Europe.

Börzel, T., & Risse, T. (2000). When Europe hits home: Europeanization and domestic change. *European Integration On-Line Papers*, *5*, 15.

Borrás, S., & Radaelli, C. (2011). The politics of governance architectures: creation, change and effects of the EU Lisbon strategy. *Journal of European Public Policy*, *18*(4), 463–484.

Bruno, I., Jacquot, S., & Mandin, L. (2006). Europeanization through its instrumentation: Benchmarking, mainstreaming and the open method of co-ordination . . . toolbox or Pandora's box?. *Journal of European Public Policy*, *13*(4), 519–536.

Busse, J. (2008, December 17–19). The role of transnational municipal networks in the governance of global climate change. In *Proceedings of the fourth annual international graduate student conference in political science*, Jerusalem (Israel).

CAE. (2016). *Cultural networking Europe, today & tomorrow, a reader*. Council of Europe Publishing.

COE. (2002). *Networking culture, the role of European cultural networks*. Council of Europe Publishing.

Cram, L. (1993). Breaking down the monolith: The European commission as multi-organizations: EC policy-making in the social policy and IT sectors. *Journal of European Public Policy*, *1*(2), 195–217.

Cram, L. (1997). The European commission and the 'European interest': Institutions, interaction and preference formation in the EU context. In *Conference paper at European Union studies association*.

Cram, L. (2011). The importance of the temporal dimension: New modes of governance as a tool of government. *Journal of European Public Policy*, *18*(5), 636–653.

Dossi, S. (2012). Urban governance encounters Europeanization: The case of the community initiative URBAN II in Bordeaux and Genoa. *Regional & Federal Studies*, *22*(2), 159–175.

De Greef, H. (2008). Give, get or get off! Challenges of cultural networking today", Brussels, European Festival Association.

EFA. (2006). Give, get or get off! Challenges of cultural networking today. In *A report on the EFA/ISPA conference Cultural Networks at work*, Brussels, 8 June 2007.

ENCATC. (2017). *The story on ENCATC, 25th years of cultural management and policy in Europe*. ENCATC.

Gerritsen, A. (2016). Domesticating goods from overseas: global material culture in the early modern Netherlands. *Journal of Design History*, *29*(3), 228–244.

Giest, S., & Howlett, M. (2013). Comparative climate change governance: Lessons from European transnational municipal network management efforts. *Environmental Policy and Governance*, *23*, 341–353.

Hass, P. (Ed.) (1992). *Knowledge, power and international coordination*. University of South Carolina Press.

IETM, Fitzcarraldo Foundation, Arts Council of Finland. (2001). *How networking work?* IETM Study on the Effects of Networking.

IFFACCA. (2016). *D'Art 49: International cultural networks*. Report.

Jacobssonn, K. (2004). Soft regulation and the subtle transformation of states: The case of EU employment policy. *Journal of European Social Policy, 14*(4).

Jacquot, S., & Woll, C. (2003). Usage of European integration – Europeanisation from a sociological perspective. *European Integration online Papers (EIoP), 7*(12).

Jacquot, S., & Woll, C. (2004). *Les usages de l'Europe acteurs et transformations européennes*. L'Harmattan.

Jacquot, S., & Woll, C. (2010). Using Europe: Strategic action in multi-level politics. *Comparative European Politics, 8*, 110–126.

Kaiser, W. (2015). Clash of cultures: Two milieus in the European Union's 'A new narrative for Europe' project'. *Journal of Contemporary European Studies, 23*(3), 364–377.

Kern, K., & Bulkeley, H. (2009). Cities, Europeanization and multi-level governance: governing climate change through transnational municipal networks. *JCMS Journal of Common Market Studies, 47*, 309–332.

Lähdesmäki, T. (2016). Politics of tangibility, intangibility and place in the making of a European cultural heritage in EU heritage policy. *International Journal of Heritage Studies, 22*(10), 766–780.

Lähdesmäki, T., Mäkinen, K., Čeginskas, V., & Kaasik-Krogerus, S. (Eds.). (2021). *Europe from below*. Brill.

Lähdesmäki, T., Thomas, S., Zhu, Y., & Suzie, T. (Eds.). (2019). *Politics of scale: New directions in critical heritage studies*. Berghahn Books.

Littoz-Monnet, A. (2012). Agenda-setting dynamics at the EU level: The case of the EU cultural policy. *Journal of European Integration, 34*(5), 505–522.

Lombardo, E., & Forest, M. (2015). The Europeanization of gender equality policies: A discursive-sociological approach. *Comparative European Politics, 13*, 222–239.

Malandrino, A. (2020). The relevance of transnational policy networks to the social and labor policy cycle in the European Union: A case study. *Politiche Sociali, 3*.

Mattocks, K. (2018). Just describing is not enough: Policy learning, transfer, and the limits of best practices. *The Journal of Arts Management, Law, and Society, 48*(2), 85–97.

Provan, K. G., & Milward, H. B. (2001). Do networks really work? A framework for evaluating public-sector organizational networks. *Public Administration Review, 61*(4), 414–423.

Pureber, T. (2022). *How to build networks and why. From resilience towards sustainability*. Kooperativa.

Radaelli, C. M. (2000). Whither Europeanization? Concept stretching and substantive change. *European Integration Online Papers (EIoP), 4*(8).

Radaelli, C. M. (2004). Europeanization: solution or problem? in *European integration on-line papers* (Vol. 8, p. 16). http://papers.ssrn.com/sol3/papers.cfm?abstract_id=601163.

Radaelli, C. M. (2008). Europeanization, policy learning, and new modes of governance. *Journal of Comparative Policy Analysis: Research and Practice, 10*(3), 239–254.

Sassatelli, M. (2010). European identity between flows and places: Insights from emerging European landscape policies. *Sociology, 44*(1).

Schmitt, T. (2009). Global cultural governance. Decision-making concerning world heritage between politics and science. *Erkunde, 63*(2), 103–121.

Schmidt, V. A. (2002). Does discourse matter in the politics of welfare state adjustment? *Comparative Political Studies, 35*(2), 168–193.

Schmidt, V. A. (2008). Discursive institutionalism: The explanatory power of ideas and discourse. *Annual Review of Political Science, 11*, 303–326.

Schmidt, V. A. (2015). *Discursive institutionalism: The explanatory power of ideas and discourse*. Cambridge University Press.

Schmidt, V. A. (2018). Rethinking EU governance: From 'old' to 'new' approaches to who steers integration. *Journal of Common Market Studies, Special Issue.*

Schmidt, V., & Radaelli, C. (2004). Policy change and discourse in Europe: conceptual and methodological issues. *West European Politics, 27*(2), 183–210.

Shore, C. (2002). The cultural policies of the European Union and cultural diversity. In Bennett, T. (Ed.), *Differing diversities. Transversal study on the theme of cultural policy and cultural diversity*. Council of Europe Publishing.

3 Driving innovation in cultural management

Lluís Bonet

3.1 Creativity versus innovation

Much has been written about the profiles, functions, and competences that a cultural manager usually possesses (Fitzgibbon & Kelly, 1997; Dalborg & Lofgren, 2016; DeVereaux, 2019), even from a rather critical approach (Brkić, 2019). Although this professional figure may have several levels of responsibility, from senior management to merely operational responsibilities, in most cases, this professional must guarantee the sustainability of a project, department or institution for which it is responsible. One of its main functions is that of mediator between the artistic or heritage proposal, the audiences, and the community (Bonet, 2010). And to make a project sustainable over time, it is necessary to foster a climate of permanent innovation (Bakhshi & Throsby, 2010). For this reason, a cultural manager must know how to encourage the creative capacity of all team members, external collaborators, and audiences and be able to transform this creativity into innovation processes.

Creativity is consubstantial to the artistic process, but it would be a mistake to consider it an exclusive attribute of creators of symbolic or artistic content, and not possessed by staff or other professionals who collaborate so that projects become a reality. There is, therefore, a compartmentalisation of functions between creative and non-creative work (Fitzgibbon, 2001), without considering that creativity is a natural attribute of any human being, the ability to imagine and develop new ideas, knowledge, meanings, or processes. It is an attribute that adds value to any social process, including the management of culture. However, cultural institutions are not always different from other institutions located in the same territory or under the same social value system. Therefore, this attribute is not always promoted by managers, and by society in general, as a factor that can transform into innovation.

Creativity is amplified when conditions are created that encourage curiosity and the freedom to think and express oneself in an original way (Van Damme et al., 2018). There are organisations that promote it, and others that don't. Even in situations in which the official rhetoric is favourable to the promotion of the creativity of the staff or the users, the practice of the organisation

DOI: 10.4324/9781003594413-3

is often not open to creativity coming from the non-creative departments of the organisation. One might think that cultural organisations are more open than other organisations, but this is not always the case.

There are societies where creativity is considered a positive social value, a seed that is worth being encouraged (Von Hippel, 2005). Others are more hierarchical or authoritarian, in which questioning the social, religious, economic, scientific, or even artistic status quo is perceived as something dangerous; and, therefore, not encouraged, restricted, or even persecuted. As a result, most creative ideas do not materialise for a combination of reasons:

- adverse social, political, economic context;
- lack of material resources for its development, implementation, and dissemination;
- technological gap between the idea, its productive materialisation, and its social acceptance;
- creators' difficulty to transform their creativity into products or real processes.

But creativity alone doesn't presuppose implementation or adding to social value. It must be transformed into innovation, "the process by which, based on creativity, new value is added to a product (good or service) or to the process of its production/distribution. Value can be exchange value (e.g. money) or use value (something useful for society, for some institutions, for some organisation, for the individual, or for a collective of individuals)" (Castells, 2017, p. 16).

Every innovation process starts from embryonic creative ideas, ideas that must be developed so that they mature, become known, and, occasionally, transform into viable novel products or processes at a social or market level. However, this is a difficult and risky process, a fact that generates caution on the part of potential investors, even though it is fashionable to talk about innovation, creative entrepreneurship, and start-ups. Also, creative people do not always have the ability to transform their ideas into innovative products or processes. In general, innovation is a process resulting from teamwork and where the confluence of artistic, social, and economic logics is crucial. Cross-fertilisation is a key to obtain good results. It is not surprising, then, that in the most innovative ecosystems, there is confluence and cooperation, the so-called triple helix of innovation, between research and academic institutions, governmental agencies giving support, and the industry (Etzkowitz, 2008). The interaction and the emergence of new hybrid platforms, such as science parks or technology transfer offices, or in the case of arts and culture, artistic residences, or creative factories, facilitate cross-fertilisation. However, alignment is not always easy since there is resistance to accepting open innovation processes given the search for temporary monopolies that seek to make a profit – and not share – the effort involved in consolidating an innovation.

Another frequent confusion consists in considering that practically all innovations come from the implementation of technological advances, mostly digital (or currently generated by artificial intelligence). Technology is an important driver of innovation, but it is not the only or necessarily the most powerful. In general, innovation appears when a diversity of social, technological, and management processes are combined (Potts, 2007). The history of innovative processes in the field of cultural management is full of this combination of factors. However, these alternative forms of innovation are often hidden from conventional assessment indicators, a phenomenon that particularly affects the cultural and creative industries (Miles & Green, 2008).

3.2 Innovation in the cultural ecosystem field

In the field of cultural innovation, as in so many others, there are multiple stereotypes. One of them states that expressions of traditional culture do not incorporate or are characterised by their capacity for innovation. In my country, Catalonia, there is a manifestation of traditional culture known as human towers or *castellers*. In recent decades, it has enjoyed surprising success, being the expression of traditional culture that has probably grown the most in terms of groups and individual practitioners, face-to-face and virtual followers, and international recognition. Its success is linked to its ability to innovate and renew itself. In an activity where physical strength a priori seems to be a determining factor, the incorporation of women has allowed it to go further and reach further. More people in the groups, more talent, and more sizes to choose from and combine, seeking the ideal alignments of the structures with the combinations of commitment, technique, height, and weight. And this, in human structures with very close physical contact. Physical and biological analysis, such as studying muscle mass and bone structure, has been used to assign the most suitable individuals to specific tasks and locations withing the castle, and video and drone recording enables detailed study and train to reduce the assembly time of the human tower. Another social innovation is the progressive incorporation of members of other cultural backgrounds, an uncommon fact in manifestations of traditional culture. Both social innovations were not made or expanded immediately. It was necessary to incorporate social mediation to break taboos and integrate immigrants into traditionally closed collectives, some of which exhibited a certain machismo and ethnocentrism. It took a lot of courage initially in the face of social pressure to the contrary, but the leaders of the groups that started these processes ended up convincing the other groups due to the good results.

This and other examples allow us to analyse the ecosystem of innovation in manifestations, production, and cultural experiences. Although the cultural sector is undoubtedly creative, with some even claiming it to be the most innovative despite lacking empirical evidence, there are specific challenges that can hinder the transformation of great ideas into actual innovation (see Figure 3.1):

- the limitation of available financial resources, associated with the difficulty of measuring the risk of investing in cultural products, a fact that ends up explaining the over-supply and self-exploitation of most unknown artists (Bakhshi & Throsby, 2010);
- fragmentation in small and medium-sized enterprises (Jones et al., 2004), with self-employed and/or part-time workers, where innovation is vital for their survival (Caves, 2000; Stam, et al., 2008). However, fragmentation is expression and guarantees the much-needed cultural diversity. In addition, small teams and organisations are more agile, adapt better to change, and detect and correct errors more quickly when they need to achieve results to survive;
- a high expressive value where ideas exploitation does not necessarily reflect production costs (DCMS, 1998; Potts et al., 2008);
- the symbolic, experiential, and/or non-utilitarian, where aesthetics play an expressive role (Caves, 2000), has the consequence that consumers evaluate, accept, and reject cultural products in a completely different way versus utilitarian products or with rational purchase theory (Stam et al., 2008);
- more than a lack of management skills (Marcella & Rowley, 2014) or the difficulty in attracting the most competent managers, the discipline of the balance sheet is missing when the objective pursued is not to maximise profits but to achieve the maximum result and social impact.

These factors need to be addressed in a nuanced manner given the divergences in innovation along the cultural industries' value chain (Brandello & Kloosterman, 2010). Some subsectors are more related to technological innovation than others, so they have a different innovation process and other management practices (Knight & Harvey, 2015).

Traditionally, in the cycle of the cultural value chain, innovation has been central to the initial creation process. Artists and curators of artistic processes know that without novelty it is very difficult to emerge in very competitive art markets, where the demanding and critical gaze of experts, programmers, and ultimately the peers is fundamental (Castañer & Campos, 2002).

One of the functions of the cultural manager is to push the creatives so that their proposals produce a positive response. But it is not just about creating recognition or promoting a new aesthetic or symbolic value, but about transmitting emotions, and knowing how to do it from a sustainable perspective. However, the innovation process does not only concern the process of artistic creation but includes the phases of production and distribution, and all the tasks associated with them – from logistics or the search for funding to communication and accountability. Innovation can be crucial to achieving the success of a project and the long-term sustainability of an organisation.

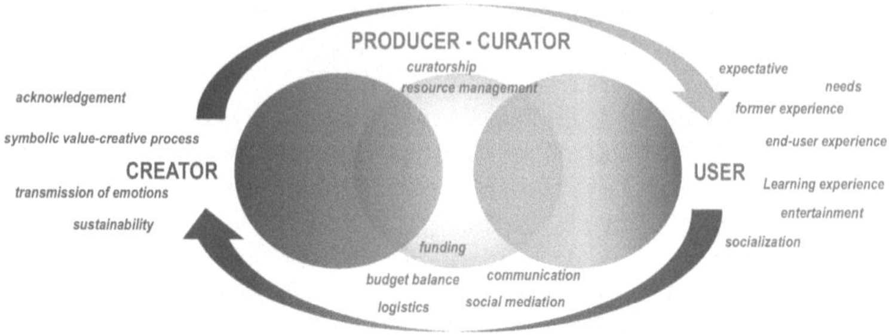

Figure 3.1 Innovation in the culture value chain ecosystem. Source: own elaboration.

An area that has gained momentum in recent years has been the transformation of the processes of reception and consumption of cultural proposals thanks to the implementation of innovations. Innovation in the experience of the user, who is not just an anonymous viewer or final receiver, but someone who adds value and is essential for the whole cultural process to make sense (Matarasso, 2019). You can innovate in the analysis of latent needs, in the process of creating expectations, and in the transformation of memories. And all these interactively.

As Schumpeter pointed out in his seminal writings on innovation (Schumpeter, 1934), in order to excel, organisations constantly seek to create new combinations of processes or products, and rival organisations try to develop their competencies by imitating or trying to improve these processes and products. The key is that innovation is difficult to imitate, and this is usually only possible when capabilities are built, such as organisational changes, and leadership models that combine the ability to attract talent with a good work environment. In the field of cultural organisations, this is even more momentous given the egos and insecurities of many creative talents, the intangibility of most products, and the scarcity of available financial resources, which translates into few financial incentives that support symbolic initiatives.

3.3 The role of the cultural manager as driver of innovation

In a milieu with many different players involved, the role of the cultural manager is to encourage all these folks to develop their creativity and innovation capacity. Many innovations involve changes in perceived meaning, new formats, or functionalities, and even changes in management and business models. So, four intertwined areas of innovation can be observed in the field of culture, which cultural management has the ability to influence:

- artistic/heritage concept;
- meaningful experience;

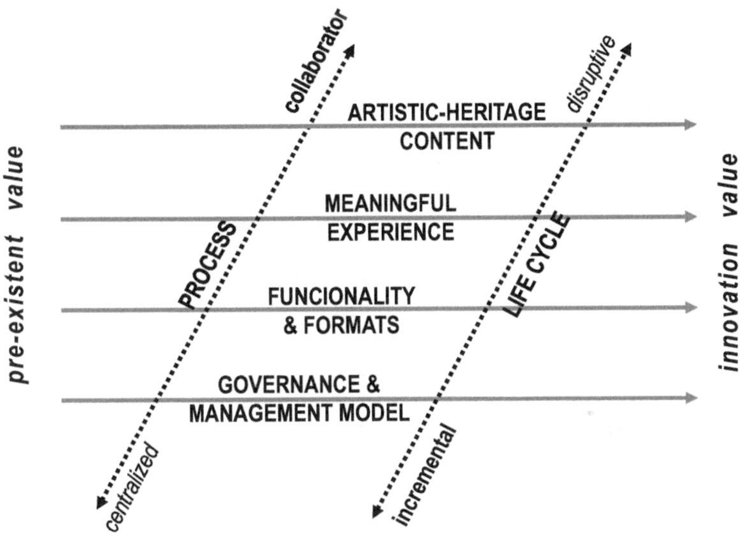

Figure 3.2 Four areas of innovation in the cultural sector. Source: own elaboration.

- functionality/format; and
- governance and management model.

Figure 3.2 summarises each of these dimensions and the intersections between them, as well as the typology of the process, the degree of centralisation and collaboration, and the life cycle of the innovation dynamic, from slow incremental innovation to disruptive. The bold or the italic text attempts to describe how often these innovation formats actually occur. Most innovative processes in the cultural field are not disruptive but are the result of a progressive process, where small steps connect one to the other. Since this takes place in open environments, professionals and organisations are inspired or adapt to each other (Powell, 2016).

It is also important to evaluate the role of the different actors when recognising, or not, the value that innovation brings, since a great idea does not always appear at the appropriate time to be socially accepted. The main beneficiary of innovation is usually the audience, which is at the same time the one who legitimises the creation of value with its presence and acceptance. But in artistic creation or in the generation of meaning, the community of experts also plays a relevant role, starting with the producers who take risks, the members of the committees that evaluate the public or private support, the programmers or curators, and the art critics. And, as far as business and management models are concerned, the response of influential actors is crucial.

Artistic creation triggers a set of processes in which different professionals (producers, curators, programmers, educators, mediators, or conservators) will contribute their knowledge and innovative capacity so that the final recipient (current or future user) can benefit from the value generated.

But as has already been mentioned, artistic creativity is not the only innovative contribution that occurs in the cultural field. Other forms of creativity coexist with it and can be transformed into innovation through participation and collaboration with other professionals, all influenced by contributions from the logic of management and cultural mediation: the creation of new meanings in the cultural experience, new formats or improved functionalities, and the creation of new business or management models. Often, an innovation involves more than one of these dimensions or areas.

The proposals that innovate in the perceived meaning of a product or cultural experience are, along with those born from artistic creativity, those that provide the greatest symbolic value. Its contribution in terms of innovation must be evaluated not only based on the intrinsic value provided but also in relation to the time passed since its initial implementation, its social acceptance, and its capacity for expansion or replication by other cultural projects. Consider, for example, the first time that a festival or a theatre left the selection of programming in the hands of a willing group of citizens instead of a professional artistic director (Bonet, Calvano, Carnelli, Dupin-Meynard & Négrier, 2018). The exhibition format could be the same but the meaning of attending a festival curated by your neighbours is totally different. Or when a museum decided to open its reserves for the first time to the general audience, instead of only to experts, with the aim of making known the wealth of the deposited fund and the multiple readings and possibilities of future exhibition. The Night of museums, the open atelier weekend, or the Music Day on the 21 June were new events that changed perception and attracted new audiences to consolidated venues. Even to propose a special setting for taking selfies, as a new way to take ownership of a monument or a landscape. In other cases, the significance of the experience is realised through activities aligned with emerging societal values (green, solidarity, and MeToo). Planning new meanings can be perceived as risky by traditional programmers or loyal audiences who enjoy the same old thing. Thanks to the imagination and skill of innovative managers, audiences today can enjoy cultural experiences with much greater meaning.

Another way to innovate is by transforming product formats or audience perception. Formats that are now fully established (i.e. the audiobook, listening to music in streaming, the QR sings or exhibition audio guides, subtitling in the performing arts, shows hosted by a DJ, or mini-theatre plays of less than 15 minutes) were surprising novelties at the time. Some innovations in format also lead to changes in perception and meaning, such as virtual or augmented reality experiences, playing video games in virtual communities, as well as remixes that involve processes of deconstruction and reconstruction. One of the most innovative formats that does not depend on a technological application is the temporary artistic residency, a very common practice today but was almost non-existent a couple of decades ago. The residencies have transformed co-production formats and the interaction between creators, venues, and their respective local audiences and communities. Not only do they provide additional economic, technical, and infrastructural resources to artists and companies, but they can transform the artistic proposal itself, thanks to the interaction with the context and its communities. Even today, implementing new formats implies a challenge and important innovation for many cultural projects, but the first to experience it deserves the merit of having taken the risk.

Finally, there are notable cases of innovation focused on the transformation of the business model and management practices. Even during the Baroque period, Italian-style theatre allowed for spatial price discrimination by offering different prices for different areas, based on the price elasticity of demand, thereby maximizing both revenue and room occupancy. Throughout the 20th century, numerous innovations in management – sometimes adaptations to the cultural field of business models from other sectors – have made it possible to make a greater number of cultural experiences a reality and make them available to citizens. For example, international co-production in cinema, exhibitions, or shows made it possible not only to share experiences and artistic and financial resources but also to expand access to new markets and complementary sources of financing.

The first years of the 21st century have been very fruitful, since technological change has forced the replacement of many old business models and has allowed the implementation of new management tools. Thus, archaic collaboration practices have gained strength and have been transformed thanks to the launch of crowdfunding or crowdsourcing platforms through the Internet. In both cases, financial, relational, or productive resources are expanded in particularly democratising production-user alliances. Some of the largest Internet platforms, such as YouTube, Instagram, or TikTok, have managed to monetise amateur artistic practices (photos, videos, and texts). On the other hand, Freemium business models (free and premium) make it possible to reach market sizes that attract massive audiences to the basic version, often with advertising, with paid services for the most demanding functionalities, and at the same time attract resources, both from advertising and from the content owners themselves. However, all these digital platform models result in an oligopolistic concentration of the market in very few hands. This is a general characteristic of the entire digital economy, where the offer of flexible prices linked to fluctuations in demand or experience designs is becoming established in many areas of the leisure and tourism sector.

For its part, audience development is also experiencing a great revolution. The analysis of participation microdata allows the programmer to know better the habits, desires, and behaviours of their audiences. If at the beginning, online ticketing relegated telephone or box office sales and allowed the public to select the offer that best suited the desired quality price, the current analysis of purchases allows promoters to better know the behaviours of their audiences, propose specific products for each person, and design targeted marketing strategies with offers and flexible subscription models based on the aggregate analysis of previous consumption. New artificial intelligence applications enable increasingly sophisticated algorithms to engage with audiences. Other applications, such as wristbands, used by a growing number of massive events and festivals, allow a secure means of payment for the user, and a source of information on the movements of the audience and types of consumption, allowing cultural managers to adjust the spatial-temporal programming and propose complementary value offers.

Another question of enormous importance is who benefits (or harms) and how the value creation of an innovation is perceived. All change creates winners and losers. Nevertheless, those innovations that generate much more profit than losses, or that the damages can be socialised or compensated in some way, bring greater social value. This is not always the case, but it is important to know how to accompany these processes, especially when the injured parties are the weakest link in the chain. Copyright protection societies were established not only to defend the economic and moral rights of creators, particularly the most successful ones, but in many countries' legislation, they are also obligated to protect the rights of less successful creators and ensure the overall welfare of all creators. It is in this balance that socially it makes sense to limit everyone's free access to culture by remunerating copyright in a temporary monopoly. Similarly, in the management of culture where most innovation processes are open, the temporary monopoly that every investor seeks is limited by the replication of successful models adapted to each reality and local context.

3.4 Dissemination and scalability of cultural innovation

One of the great challenges of innovation in the cultural sector is the limited capacity to achieve greater dissemination; that is, to scale in dimension and impact. The uniqueness of most projects, the importance of the local and regional context, the personality of the professionals who have made it possible, or the scarcity of resources available to invest are some of the reasons that explain the limited dissemination of many innovative proposals. To these specific aspects, three additional general factors should be added: (a) the speed of expansion of the innovation, which is inversely proportional to the ability to control the adoption by third parties of the innovation, as shown in the practices described in Figure 3.3; (b) the ability for the first implementers of the idea to control the process of its social dissemination; and (c) the model of value monetisation and return on investment generated with the process of its expansion and dissemination.

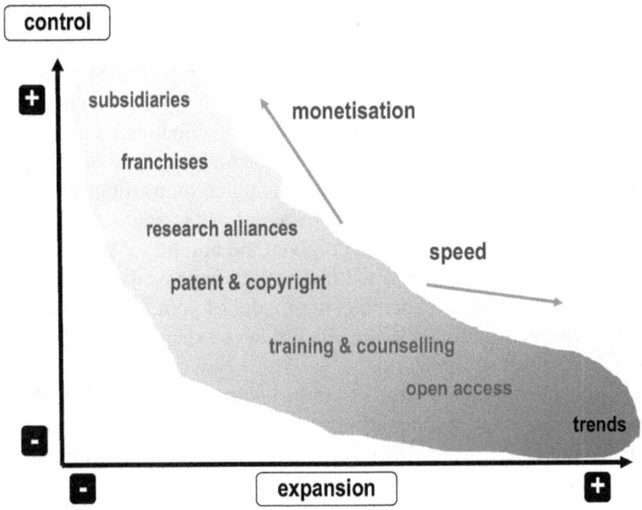

Figure 3.3 Models of innovation expansion. Source: own elaboration.

In closed innovation processes, the most common way to expand an innovation consists of the creation of subsidiaries or expansion via franchising. Subsidiaries provide more control but require greater investment by the parent company. In the cultural field, there are more examples of franchises than of companies with subsidiaries, but there are quite successful cases such as artistic training schools, focused on the prestige of the brand and the applied pedagogical methodology, or the international expansion of architecture studios like the Norwegian studio Snøhetta, with offices in many different cities around the globe.

In contrast, franchised systems rely on investment and a network of local contacts. The license to use the name, advice, and initial training are granted, in exchange for a financial return, and maintaining quality controls specified in standard contracts for the entire franchise network. In the cultural field, the practice is much more personalised; rather than talking about franchise networks, it would be about a few well-selected cases, with ad hoc contracts. The best-known cases have involved large museums (the Guggenheim and the Louvre among the best known) or prestigious festivals. In the latter case, there is a great diversity of models, not all of them strictly classifiable as franchises (because beyond simply transferring names and sharing experiences among some artists, there is a wide range of relationships, often with more emphasis on service exchanges for economic returns rather than fixed fees).

Another way to reduce the investment and risk associated with any innovation and development process is to establish alliances with other organisations to share the long and risky process of developing an innovation in the respective sectoral or geographic market. In this sense, belonging to networks enables entities to meet partners and establish shared strategies. Similarly, being part of a network of agents that share a quality certification, or a patent or copyright or reproduction rights, is also a way of disseminating an innovation. In a more informal setting, training or personalised advice have been especially efficient ways of disseminating and generalising an innovation. Finally, open innovation or being part of a certain movement or fashion is the mechanism that implies the greatest social impact, given the number of projects that can be involved. For example, one of the innovative movements with the greatest numerical and territorial expansion is the model of youth orchestras founded by maestro Abreu, initially in Venezuela but later expanded throughout Latin America and the rest of the world.

In the first models, the degree of control is much higher, while the speed and scope of expansion of innovation are much greater when they are part of movements or have been generated from access or open innovation processes. In all these cases, the value monetisation models generated by the innovation expansion process depend on the type of direct or implicit contracts that are generated and the expansion process itself (e.g. the creator of a very popular innovation can obtain more individual income through invitations and collaboration proposals than from an uncertain franchisor).

In any case, the expansion of an innovation to broader territories, where they do not compete directly for the same market or audience, is frankly desirable. Being part of a network of projects that share the same innovative process or brand, like micro-theatre, doesn't weaken its impact; rather, it enhances it. It is important, in any case, to try to contextualise the respective local area so that the project is truly viable. Those who simply copy a successful model (e.g. summer music festivals with almost identical programming and accompanying proposals beyond the change of environment and name) do not manage to innovate, but rather only copy.

3.5 Role and dilemmas of the cultural manager as a driver of innovation

In the realm of cultural management, innovation presents numerous dilemmas that challenge the traditional paradigms and practices within the sector. These dilemmas, often complex and multifaceted, require cultural managers to navigate a delicate balance between competing priorities (Jacobs & Kooyman, 2015). Some of these critical dilemmas are

a) Risk versus sustainability

Innovation inherently involves risk, pushing cultural managers to venture into uncharted territories. However, this pursuit of novelty must be weighed against the need for sustainability. While innovative projects can attract new audiences and funding, they can also threaten the long-term viability of an organisation if they fail. Cultural managers must thus strategically assess which risks are worth taking and devise contingency plans to ensure that the organisation's core mission and financial health remain intact. In the long term, the sustainability of an organisation depends on the ability to adapt and incorporate innovation throughout its life cycle, especially at critical moments, as demonstrated, for example, in the cases of *Cirque du Soleil* (Simon, 2015) or *Snøhetta* (Bonet & Rykkja, 2023).

b) Legacy versus change

Cultural organisations often have rich histories and legacies that shape their identity and public perception. Introducing change can rejuvenate these institutions, making them more relevant to contemporary audiences. However, this can also alienate existing supporters and damage the organisation's heritage. Managers must find a way to honour and preserve the legacy of their organisations while embracing change, ensuring that innovations are seen as extensions rather than disruptions of tradition.

c) Equity and social inclusion versus excellence and artistic value

The pursuit of equity and social inclusion is a fundamental ethical obligation for cultural managers, aiming to democratise access to culture. However, this can sometimes conflict with the pursuit of excellence and high artistic value, which may favour more selective or elite artistic expressions. Balancing these priorities requires a nuanced approach that promotes inclusivity without compromising the quality and integrity of artistic outputs.

d) Institutionalisation versus spontaneity

Institutionalisation provides structure, stability, and legitimacy to cultural initiatives, but it can also stifle spontaneity and creativity. Cultural managers must strike a balance, fostering an environment where institutional frameworks support but do not constrain creative expression. This might involve flexible organisational structures and processes that allow for spontaneous, innovative projects alongside more established programmes.

e) Passion and enthusiasm versus rationality and viability

The cultural sector is often driven by passion and enthusiasm, with many managers and practitioners deeply committed to their work. However, this passion must be balanced with rationality to ensure that projects are feasible and sustainable. Effective cultural management involves channelling enthusiasm into carefully planned and executed initiatives that align with the organisation's strategic goals and financial realities.

f) Consolidated prestige versus artistic emergence

Established institutions with consolidated prestige have a strong reputation and audience base, but they may struggle to remain innovative and relevant. In contrast, emerging artists and organisations often bring fresh perspectives and innovation, but lack visibility and support. Cultural managers must create platforms that both honour prestigious legacies and nurture artistic emergence, ensuring a dynamic and evolving cultural landscape.

g) Cognitive effort versus entertainment

Cultural experiences can be intellectually stimulating, requiring significant cognitive effort, or they can be entertaining and easily accessible. Balancing these aspects involves understanding the diverse needs and preferences of audiences. Cultural managers should aim to offer a spectrum of experiences that engage different audience segments, from highbrow, intellectually demanding works to more accessible, entertaining pieces.

h) Cultural diplomacy versus horizontal cultural co-operation

Cultural diplomacy involves promoting a country's culture internationally to build soft power, while horizontal cultural cooperation emphasises equal partnerships and cultural exchange between communities. Cultural managers need to navigate these approaches, fostering international cultural relations that respect mutual exchange and collaboration rather than unilateral promotion. This ensures that cultural diplomacy is practiced ethically and inclusively, benefiting all parties involved.

i) Equitable access to and data interpretation by AI between large platforms and cultural organisations with different capacities/resources

The rise of artificial intelligence (AI) in cultural management offers powerful tools for audience engagement and operational efficiency. However, the access to and interpretation of AI-generated data can vary significantly between large platforms with substantial resources and smaller cultural organisations. This disparity can exacerbate existing inequalities, making it essential for cultural managers to advocate for more equitable access to AI technologies and support capacity-building initiatives within smaller organisations.

Another responsibility of the cultural manager, in their role as a social and cultural mediator, is understanding the uses and abuses of the most advanced technologies and, in particular, artificial intelligence. The more we know about the subject, the more aware we are of what we don't know, and those who use AI uncritically probably aren't aware of that. As professionals, the more prepared we are to embrace the potential of a new technology, being aware of its multiple risks, the more it can help us individually and collectively to serve the entire society. One of the most important challenges is how to manage the new "illiteracy" and social and economic bifurcation generated by the mastery (or not) of these technologies. What responsibility do we have as cultural managers in relation to our team, other cultural professionals, our audience, and the community in general?

Despite the regulatory efforts of the European Union in the field of AI, the situation is quite alarming since the new technologies reproduce the structural relationship of market dominance by the powerful – the designers and owners of the algorithms – who collect millions of bits of data and use it to configure the products and the market; often the only thing that changes over time are some of the protagonists. As recent studies show, digitisation did not reduce the concentration of the market that is in the hands of the most successful products and companies, even in the case of independent music platforms (Pilati et al., 2024). On a global scale, we see how China, with its stringent population control policies, has taken the lead in new AI patents, while the United States, despite pressure from unions, strives to maintain its dominance through global content platforms.

Navigating this long list of dilemmas requires cultural managers to be strategic, empathetic, and adaptable. They must constantly reassess their priorities and decisions to balance competing interests and values. By doing so, they can foster a vibrant, inclusive, and innovative cultural landscape that respects tradition while embracing the future. In the dynamic field of cultural management, certain leadership trends are essential for effectively fostering innovation. Leaders in this sector are encouraged to cultivate an environment where empowerment is central. This involves creating opportunities for team members to innovate, share doubts, and engage in collective learning to facilitate collaborative decision-making. Simultaneously, effective leaders demonstrate the capacity to make difficult decisions and address risks and uncomfortable issues directly (Mulcahy, 2006).

Leadership in cultural management should be conceptualised as an act of service rather than exploitation (Dragićević-Šešić & Stefanović, 2017). Managers are expected to focus on integrating team members and supporting their growth, recognising that generosity and care yield substantial long-term benefits. Success is often mirrored in a leader's ability to amplify their impact through others, fostering both personal and professional development within their team. Assembling a team of talented, curious, and committed individuals is crucial. These team members should exhibit a willingness to learn and an openness to risk, balanced with humility, and accept and learn from failures. Cultivating respect for the team, the organisation, and the broader community is vital in mitigating future mistakes and promoting a culture of continuous improvement. The principle that talent attracts talent plays a significant role in creating a cycle of excellence within the organisation (Dewey & Beebe, 2010).

Effective projects are frequently guided by leaders who possess the ability to attract and inspire other professionals. While retaining such talent is important, it is equally vital to support their pursuit of new dreams and projects, thereby expanding cooperation networks and fostering broader collaborative opportunities (Belfiore & Bennett, 2007). Managerial shared leadership makes creative organisations more resilient, transparent, open, and generous constellation (Bonet & Rykkja, 2023); traits that favour innovation within and around the organisation itself.

Managing significant egos, particularly among prominent creators, is another critical skill for cultural leaders. Ensuring that all team members feel valued and are able to perform at their best requires a delicate balance of nurturing individual talent while maintaining team cohesion (Levine, 2009). Additionally, leaders are tasked with effectively addressing the challenges posed by team members who may be demotivated, resistant to change, or less competent. Addressing grievances, fixed mindsets, and a lack of personal commitment is essential. Leaders are expected to steer such individuals away from blaming others and avoiding risk, and instead foster a culture of accountability and continuous improvement (Marcet, 2018).

By embracing these leadership trends, cultural managers can effectively drive innovation, creating dynamic, inclusive, and forward-thinking cultural environments.

3.6 Concluding remarks

The innovation ecosystem in the cultural sector has specific characteristics. Firstly, the way in which creativity is translated into innovation is complex, in that proposals are generated by both the artistic team, and other cultural professionals, technicians, managers, or entrepreneurs. One of the causes of this complexity is that artistic innovation is often the result of a much more individual and subjective drive and is promoted from a more institutional, social, or business perspective. In most cases, it is the result of open innovation processes, where the community plays a notable role.

Secondly, there is an inherent tension between, on the one hand, symbolic, identity, heritage, or aesthetic considerations, and on the other hand, political, commercial, or social aspects. From a political perspective, the empowerment of local or national culture – from heritage legacy to avant-garde creation – is an important challenge in the context of growing homogenisation and globalisation of cultural expressions and practices. But government support for the sector and its creativity is not only explained by symbolic reasons or social cohesion but also economic, since the creative economy can generate added value and employment to the extent that it can present innovative proposals. This explains the development of public policies that not only support creativity and experimentation but also try to channel it through innovation processes towards more commercial (Brandello & Kloosterman, 2010) or community results. In this last aspect, strategies to support innovation do not differ too much from policies to promote innovation in other areas. Cultural production also needs to distinguish itself from the competition, offering itself as a carrier of added value, not only in economic terms, to survive and position itself in a changing environment. This explains why even institutions that offer a standard product (a library, a museum exhibition, a concert hall, or a publishing label) must transform either their business model, the format, or the meaning of the experience offered, to continue providing social value, accessibility, and novelty. From this perspective, the role of the cultural manager is key, as it can help to convey and be a reference alongside the rest of the cultural professionals and the society in which they live.

Thirdly, the ability to generate new meanings, experiences, or knowledge, and the process by which creativity is transformed into innovation – by being transformed into goods or services that generate aesthetic, social, or economic value for its protagonists and for society as a whole – is gradual. In general, it is the result of a discontinuous incremental process. Disruptive innovation is much rarer. Figure 3.2 shows the diversity of dimensions or areas in which cultural innovation develops. As has been reiterated throughout this text, artistic creativity is not the only innovative contribution that is given, but rather it coexists with the creation of new meanings in the cultural experience, the proposal of new formats or functionalities, as well as the creation of new business or management models.

There is a great diversity of good innovation practices in the cultural field, including both government initiatives (despite the additional difficulty of innovating from bureaucratic institutions obliged to follow administrative procedures) and business-oriented initiatives in the field of social participation and non-profit organisations. In the book "Innovation in the management of culture, reflections and experiences" (Bonet & Gonzalez-Piñero, 2021), we collected many excellent examples. The key lies in the leadership of its managers since creativity is latent in the human resources of any organisation, it is only necessary to enhance it and guide it towards innovation processes.

Finally, we educators play a crucial role in turning future cultural managers into open-minded leaders. This involves fostering critical thinking and adaptability, and helping students navigate the complexities of cultural management with agility, creativity, and resourcefulness. A key aspect is the promotion of ethical responsibility and inclusion, fundamental values that cannot be left aside in social innovation processes. Experiential learning through internships and hands-on projects is essential to apply theoretical knowledge in real-world contexts. Our responsibility as educators is to inspire and support emerging professionals so that they become visionary leaders, capable of achieving impactful and sustainable results in the cultural sector. In particular, when one observes the sociological profile of the majority of students who decide to undertake careers in the field of cultural management (Dubois, 2013).

3.7 References

Bakhshi, H., & Throsby, D. (2010). *Culture of innovation: an economic analysis of innovation in arts and cultural organisations*. NESTA.

Belfiore, E., & Bennett, O. (2007). *Rethinking the social impact of the arts: A critical-historical review*. Centre for Cultural Policy Studies, University of Warwick.

Bonet, L. (Ed.). (2010). *Perfil i reptes del gestor cultural*. Gescènic.

Bonet, L., Calvano, G., Carnelli, L., Dupin-Meynard, F., & Négrier, E. (Eds.). (2018). *Be SpectACTive! 'Challenging participation in performing arts*. Editoria & Spettacolo.

Bonet, L., & Gonzalez-Piñero, M. (Eds.). (2021). *La innovación en la gestión de la cultura. Reflexiones y experiencias*. Edicions UB.

Bonet, L., & Rykkja, A. (2023). Why is managerial shared leadership in creative organizations a more resilient, transparent, open, and generous constellation? A case analysis approach. *European Journal of Cultural Management and Policy*, *13*, 12056. https://doi.org/10.3389/ejcmp.2023.12056

Brandello, A. M., & Kloosterman, R. C. (2010). Keeping the market at bay: exploring the loci of innovation in the cultural industries. *Creative Industries Journal*, *3*(1+2), 61–77.

Brkić, A. (2019). Death of the arts manager. In C. DeVereaux (Ed.), *Arts & cultural management: Sense and sensibilities in the state of the field*. Routledge.

Castañer, X., & Campos, L. (2002). The determinants of artistic innovation: Bringing in the role of organizations. *Journal of Cultural Economics*, *26*(1), 29–52.

Castells, M. (Ed.) (2017). *Another economy is possible: Culture and economy in a time of crisis*. Polity.

Dalborg, K., & Lofgren M. (2016). *Perspectives on cultural leadership. The Fika project*. Natverkstan kultur.

DCMS (1998). *Creative industries mapping document*. Department for Culture, Media and Sport.

DeVereaux, C. (Ed.). (2019). *Arts & cultural management: Sense and sensibilities in the state of the field*. Routledge.

Dewey, P., & Beebe, R. S. (2010). *Leadership in the performing arts*. Focal Press.

Dragićević-Šešić, M., & Stefanović, M. (2017). Leadership styles and values. The case of independent cultural organisations. *Cultural Management: Science & Education, 1*(1), 29.

Dubois, V. (2013). *Culture as a vocation: Sociology of career choices in cultural management*. Routledge.

Etzkowitz, H. (2008). *The triple helix: University-industry-government innovation in action*. Routledge.

Fitzgibbon, M. (2001). *Managing innovation in the arts: Making art work.* Bloomsbury Publishing USA.

Fitzgibbon, M., & Kelly, A. (Eds.). (1997). *From maestro to manager: Critical issues in arts and culture management.* Oak Tree Press.

Jacobs, R., & Kooyman, R. (2015). The entrepreneurial ant. Rethinking arts management education. In O. Kuhle, A. Schramme, & R. Kooyman (Eds.), *Creating cultural capital. Cultural entrepreneurship in theory, pedagogy and practice.* Eburon, University of Chicago Press.

Jones, C. et al. (2004). Innovation in the creative industries: The role of small and medium-sized enterprises. In *Creative industries and the economy: Innovation in the creative sector* (pp. 123–145). Routledge.

Knight, E., & Harvey, W. (2015). Managing exploration and exploitation paradoxes in creative organisations. *Management Decision, 53*(4), 809–827.

Levine, P. (2009). *Reclaiming the public: Community and citizenship in the age of new media.* Harvard University Press.

Marcella, R., & Rowley, J. (2014). The lack of management skills in the creative industries: A case study. *International Journal of Arts Management, 16*(3), 38–53.

Marcet, X. (2018). *Esquivar la mediocridad: Notas sobre management: Complejidad, estrategia e innovación.* Plataforma.

Matarasso, F. (2019). *A restless art. How participation won and why it matters.* Calouste Gulbenkian Foundation.

Miles, I., & Green, L. (2008). *Hidden innovation in the creative industries.* Nesta.

Mulcahy, K. V. (2006). Cultural policy: A comparative analysis of cultural policies and policy-making. The *Journal of Arts Management, Law, and Society, 35*(4), 263–278.

Potts, J. D. (2007). Art and innovation: an evolutionary economic view of the creative industry. *The UNESCO Observatory, 1*(1), 1–18.

Potts, J. D. et al. (2008) The cultural industries and evolutionary economics'. *International Journal of Cultural Policy, 14*(2), 143–158.

Powell, W. W. (2016). A sociologist looks at crowds: Innovation or invention? *Strategic Organization, 15*(2), 289–297.

Pilati, F., Houssard, A., & Sacco, P. L. (2024). Mirroring the inequalities of mainstream music platforms: popularity, revenue, and monetization strategies on Bandcamp. *International Journal of Cultural Policy.* https://doi.org/10.1080/10286632.2024.2356169

Schumpeter, J. A. (1934[2006]). *The theory of economic development.* Transaction Publishers.

Simon, L. (2015). Setting the stage for collaborative creative leadership at Cirque du Soleil. *Technology Innovation Management Review, 12*(1), 47–58.

Stam, E., De Jong, J. P. J., & Martel, G. (2008). Entrepreneurship, innovation, and regional development: The role of self-employed and part-time workers. *Regional Studies, 42*(7), 923–934.

Van Damme, I., De Munck, B., & Miles, A. (2018). *Cities and creativity from the renaissance to the present.* Routledge.

Von Hippel, E. (2005). *Democratizing innovation.* The MIT Press.

Index

Note: Page numbers in *italics* indicate a figure on the corresponding page.